VET
NOIR

VET NOIR

It's not the Pets—it's the People Who Make Me Crazy

Robin Truelove Stronk DVM

iUniverse, Inc.
New York   Bloomington

VET NOIR

It's not the Pets—it's the People Who Make Me Crazy

Cover photos by Rhonda MacLeod, Clear Light Photography
Illustrations by Robin Truelove Stronk DVM

iUniverse books may be ordered through booksellers or by contacting:

iUniverse
1663 Liberty Drive
Bloomington, IN 47403
www.iuniverse.com
1-800-Authors (1-800-288-4677)

ISBN: 978-1-4401-9735-2 (pbk)
ISBN: 978-1-4401-9736-9 (ebk)
ISBN: 978-1-4401-9737-6 (hbk)

Printed in the United States of America

iUniverse rev. date: 1/6/2010

CONTENTS

Veterinarians face new challenges every day, but plying my profession while sharing a bed with three other people and a cat was not one I had anticipated. Daily drama and the stress of painful decisions make the job difficult at best and sometimes undermine my best effort. I discovered my required safety net in the black humor of my internal monologue.

Every institution has its legends, and Dr. Fox was one of the most intimidating at the veterinary college at Cornell University. As one of only six women in his Large Animal Medicine class, I experienced his verbal tirades and scathing critiques, which were satisfyingly unbiased. Nobody escaped his winnowing fork.

My karma seemed to be affecting me inappropriately. I was the only female in a laboratory class in reproductive studies. Our group mission was to collect a semen sample from an unsuspecting Beagle. My maiden name is Truelove. This irony was not wasted on the crowd.

Clothes may make the man, but we thought that hats would make us viable veterinary candidates. Our first bovine patients restructured our way of thinking.

Everything at the veterinary school was exciting and new. I experienced many challenging situations including an impromptu striptease accompanied by a simian patient in front of a waiting room packed with delighted onlookers. I did not enjoy the spotlight.

Why did the loud command, "Run!" always accompany my interactions with pigs? From my work in a feedlot in school with a professor who heroically attempted to keep us on our feet, to my confrontation with a pet pig that slept on his owners' bed and had to be controlled by metering out Cheerios, I realized I was not meant for pig practice.

New England farmers have reasonable expectations. In my experience, they expected me to show up when summoned, have a good knowledge of bovine medicine, and give them value for their money. Unfortunately, some also had a few unreasonable expectations, like being prepared to see me strip to the waist to assist in a difficult calving.

Animals are creatures of the moment. Liberated from concerns about their personal finances, the world situation, or their battle with their weight, they are free to focus on one concept. When their pursuit of emancipation clashes with my need to contain them, I enter the lightning round of decision-making. The Great Race ensues.

Pride is a cruel mistress. As a young practitioner, I was eager to please. I sometimes let my bravado overstep my experience level when it came to client relations. Apparently, we all hear the siren call of self-satisfaction and we all must pay the price.

Students who accompanied us to experience life in veterinary practice could be stimulating, helpful, and occasionally frustrating. This one seemed invisible. My overzealous attempt to win over a new stable client led to a mortifying loss of my dignity in front of the assembled crowd. My invisible assistant was the only one who could tell the tale and she had gone missing.

I was faced with one of the most literal human beings that I had ever interrogated on one of the most perplexing cases I had experienced. I soon found that attempts to extract information from the equine patient would be more fruitful than further questioning of the owner, a man of very, very few words.

What were people thinking? Before the days of caller ID, the telephone could be anonymous. I received phone calls in my career that caused me to blush and fall speechless. I dealt with each one in the most professional way that I could. I was more successful with some than I was with others.

A Saturday night spent clinging to the hitch of a tractor driven by an inebriated farmer sent us careering through a wall of thorn bushes to face an irate cow that eventually tried to pound us into the mud. Not exactly a tried and true recipe for romance, and yet I still fell for him.

A bereaved family needed help with the disposal of their beloved pet pony after I had euthanized it. Once the task was accepted, my day degenerated through various levels of despair into the macabre.

When a part time position became available at Quinnipiac University, I had to follow a nagging ambition to teach. By the time I was through with my second semester, I realized that ignoring that inner voice the rest of my life would have been much easier.

Veterinary school prepared me for the medical and surgical challenges I would face in the field. Unfortunately, that preparation ended at the animal's care and made little mention of means of remuneration for our efforts. My husband and I had to manage creatively our clients' need for our services when they were unable to pay. If only we could have hosted our own *Antiques Road Show*, we may have been able to retire earlier.

Graduating in 1975, I firmly believed that indeed, I *was* woman and that they *would* hear me roar. Figuring out the logistics of veterinary practice while dealing with pregnancy and then finding that it just got worse after the child became a separate, demanding entity with its own agenda (and sense of humor) revealed a necessarily mellower self-image

At 2:00 AM, a client tried to entice me to communicate with her ill guinea pig on the telephone. My refusal led to a most interesting emergency examination and a lovely hostess gift. The guinea pig owner became a cherished client and her eccentric ways became part of the fabric of daily practice.

New associates brought new ideas, new challenges, and sometimes-new odors. Dr. Dan was charming but awkward. His first night on emergency duty was a classic event full of pathos and drama when I almost misdiagnosed a critical patient after misunderstanding a sign that had actually emanated from my associate rather than the dog on the surgery table.

Dr. Steve was an experienced practitioner when he joined our practice. One of our most notorious patients, a veritable canine garbage disposal, presented to him with the usual suspect   symptoms. We all knew something was wedged in his gut, we just didn't know exactly what.

After a long frustrating search for the ideal vacuum cleaner, my prayers seemed to have been answered when a tearful client appeared at the clinic with her injured cat. Although I never did find the "Vacuum Supreme," I garnered enough information from the case to terrify a Kirby sales representative and send him fleeing from my home.

An elderly client brought his cat in for an emergency examination. After pondering the situation, I suddenly realized that I was treating the wrong patient. He would not be convinced until I confronted him with the bloody evidence.

Fainting is nature's way of telling us that our brain has received some kind of sensory overload and needs to shut down for a while. There is never a convenient time for this in a veterinary clinic. Clients faint, technicians faint, even doctors faint.

Some stories are so saccharine that I am reluctant to tell them and yet they must be told because they are true. We must learn from history. We must be cautious with our goodies. And most importantly, we should think very carefully when naming our pets.

My new clients had arrived filled with veterinary knowledge and lore gleaned from their zealous devotion to *Emergency Vets* on television. My personal bubble of superiority burst when I realized that their suspicions were more on target than mine were. After a successful outcome to their pet's surgery, I couldn't imagine why the wife became suddenly morose.

You always hurt the one you love. The most aggravating request that clients consistently make of me sets my teeth grinding. I most definitely *would* mind!

At last, I think I've found my ideal practice situation. Treating animals without dealing with their owners should be the easiest task I've had. So I thought, until treating Edgar Allen Crow and a host of other Good Samaritan cases.

After more than thirty years as a veterinarian, I now realize that a large part of my career involves the care and maintenance of Homo sapiens. I received no preparation for the people in the animals' lives. They have been kind beyond measure, awesomely dedicated, and splendidly appreciative over the years. They have also been quirky, infuriating, and sometimes behaved in totally inexplicable fashion.

CHAPTER 1
How Do You Do That?

Reclining on the king-size bed in the semidarkness, I leaned closer to my husband's ear and quietly asked him to adjust the light on the night table. We weren't alone. I looked at the couple who shared the bed with us and tried to discern their thoughts. The only sound was the low-pitched purr emanating from their three-legged cat nestled in the center of their bed. The couple seemed to be maintaining their emotional equilibrium. My stability, however, was a little shaky.

How did I come to be sharing a bed with my husband, two clients, and their mortally ill cat?

As a veterinarian, my mission on this particular day was sad. The mechanics of the process were simple. I had performed it hundreds of times before and felt confident in my ability. The emotional aspect, however, was daunting. I struggled to find the most compassionate words to ease this couple through their loss as I prepared to euthanize their beloved pet. In veterinary school, there had been no textbook on my list of required reading and only anecdotal information from our professors to guide me. Yet, I had found that the real measure of my worth as a veterinarian was what I could do not only for the pet, but also for the owners, in the next few minutes and even on into the next few weeks.

This case had started out unremarkably. A middle-aged couple with no children had presented their older cat for an examination at my clinic. She had been lame for a few days. I determined that the cat had pain in one of her hips, and I recommended an X-ray. To my dismay, I found that the geriatric patient had an unusual form of bone cancer in her hip. Ultimately, her leg was amputated in an attempt to stop the painful progression of the disease, but despite all efforts, it metastasized to her lungs. At that point, the treatment options were exhausted, and we kept her as comfortable as possible until the time came when the owners felt her quality of life did not warrant taking her any farther.

I was genuinely fond of the couple. The clients who I affectionately categorize as my "cat people" are very special. We tell silly cat stories in the exam room, matching one another in self-deprecating descriptions of the depths to which we will lower ourselves to accommodate our kitties. We all understand that our cats see us as heated furniture, which explains their preference for lying on our lap rather than in a more convenient location.

The wife enjoyed spinning yarn. One winter she had come into the clinic sporting a gorgeous soft-knitted hat. She proudly explained that the buff-colored top and brim had been made of yarn she had spun from the hair she combed from her young, longhaired orange tabby. The gray band at the edge of the brim was from the hair combed from her older, shorthaired gray tiger. The hat was truly a labor of love and most remarkable.

Now I was faced with ending the life and the physical bond between the owners and this cat that was memorialized in the hat. Veterinarians face such dilemmas on a weekly or even daily basis. On some really bad days, we may have to repeat such a scenario more than once in a day. I am not sure how others manage their emotional equilibrium, but personally, I have held to my belief that "If it weren't for black humor, we would have no humor at all." I never lose sight of the human suffering, and certainly not the animals' suffering, but I preserve my personal stability by trying to appreciate some of the irony the bad times present. Caregiver's burnout is a very real problem in our profession and cannot only sabotage our quality of work, but can ultimately end a career prematurely. We need to have our personal tools to combat it. Respectful laughter can be good medicine. When the laughter is self-directed, it doesn't even need to be respectful. To continue to function and provide support, I have to find a few hearty laughs somewhere. Exactly when they come out can be managed, but sometimes they must be stored up like energy in a battery to see me through the grim days. By acknowledging the threads of hope and joy, I can more easily endure the poignant parts of the ride.

Because my clients had been through so much emotional turmoil and their cat was now exceedingly frail, I had offered to do the euthanasia in their home. I often offered this service whenever I could to make an unwelcome situation as palatable as possible. I understand the anguish of packing the pet into the car for the last trip to the veterinary clinic. Even when they know it is the correct and humane decision, owners feel like traitors. The animal is also most stressed by the clinic environment. Although the procedure may be more technically difficult for the veterinarian, going to the patient's home and allowing them to slip from life in a comfortable, familiar environment can truly be a gift. Many times, the owner will fixate on the last image of their pet, and if they see the dog laying quietly in his usual bed in the living room it is so much better than an eternal image of his poor lifeless body on a cold steel table. Usually we work under conditions that are far from ideal, but it is worth the sacrifice. This event qualified as one of the less idyllic in my experience.

My patient had been too weak to walk very far for several days, and the owners had allowed her to stay in a nest of blankets in the middle of their king-size bed. They asked if I could perform the procedure without moving her. I agreed without reservation. Noticing their younger cat prowling and looking around, I suggested ahead of time that they confine him to another part of the house so there would be no distractions. Because I was sure that my large doctor's bag must carry odors of the clinic, I decided to leave it in the living room, not wanting to upset my patient in any way. I opened the bag, selected what I needed, and adjourned to the bedroom, closing the door to keep the other inquisitive feline out.

The owners again asked if I minded leaving the cat where she was and I again promised we would disturb her as little as possible. They wanted to lie with the cat on the bed to comfort her in her last moments, which I had anticipated and encouraged them to do. I always bring someone to assist me in these cases to help ensure that all will go smoothly. Since this was a particularly delicate and somewhat personal situation, my husband and partner in the clinic, had agreed to come to support the patient and hold her leg for me to administer the solution. Gently, we both eased ourselves down on the bed, adjusting ourselves so that we could both obtain adequate access to the patient while being careful not to intrude on the owners' positions.

Immediately, I saw that my task would be challenging. The cat was so debilitated and her blood pressure was so low that no obviously accessible vein could be found. This happens in many older pets, but it can usually be handled by clipping the hair over the vein to improve its visibility. Although I hated to prolong the scene for the clients, I needed to ensure that everything would go as smoothly as possible. I explained to them that I needed to clip a small patch of fur and excused myself to get the clippers from my bag. I felt badly leaving my husband alone to support them, but I carefully slid off the bed and slipped out to the living room.

Comic relief was on the way. I entered the living room and out of my open bag, like a jack-in-the-box, popped the bewhiskered head and banner-like tail of the younger cat. Seeing my approach, he tucked himself back in and began tossing around the vials and rolls of bandage material in the bag. It was clear that he felt I had arrived bearing a technically advanced superior cat toy, and he was enjoying it thoroughly. Quickly removing him, I realized that the previously organized contents had been thoroughly mixed. Gauze rolls were snarled and the contents were in disarray. As I quickly straightened the items and disentangled the clippers, the disarmingly healthy housemate kept leaping from the back of the couch pouncing back into the bag. When the thought crept into my mind that the cat might have felt differently if he knew the real reason for my visit, I quickly pushed it away. The situation was heartrending enough without compounding the matter. I extricated the clippers, quickly closed the bag—much to the house jester's disgust—and cleared my mind for the task ahead.

Taking a deep breath to focus my thoughts, I returned to the bedroom, being sure to close the door behind me. I couldn't entertain the possibility that my furry friend would turn his attention to the event occurring on the bed.

Nothing had changed in my absence, although I sensed that the clients were having a difficult time maintaining their composure as they crooned lovingly to their pet. After clipping a small area over the vein, I again eased myself onto the bed, vying for a tenable working position without moving or lying on anyone else.

Now I realized that the lighting situation was dismal. A very small lamp on a bedside table, which at this point seemed to be miles from my patient, cast the only available glow in the room. I looked up quickly and was disappointed to see that there was no overhead lighting. As personal stress levels built up, I whispered my request to my husband to adjust the light. He knew exactly what the problem was, and he did his best with what we had to give me some small bit of illumination.

By this time, the couple's tears had started to flow. My heart was breaking for these loving owners. I could feel tears of sympathy starting to well up in my own eyes. The next inevitable stage would involve my hands starting to shake, and I knew that would be very bad. I knew that I could end up in a disastrous circumstance if I didn't pull myself together. I briefly looked up in a desperate attempt to center myself when an epiphany struck me—*Bob & Carol & Ted & Alice.*

Looking at the scene I was in, my subconscious mind had downloaded the iconic image from the hedonistic movie of 1969. Certainly, the vista before me more closely resembled that than it did a funeral, and I was instantaneously ashamed of myself for having such an inappropriate comparison pop into my mind. Like a train with no brakes, the thought went farther. Would I more resemble Natalie Wood or Dyan Cannon? That dilemma finally brought me back to reality.

The unsolicited flight of fancy had turned the tide. Filled with shame at my irreverent thoughts, I now found my hand steady, my eyes clear, and my task straightforward. I cared no less for the owners or cat than I had five minutes before, and I felt no less sadness over their plight. It was just that now I was able to put enough distance between the situation and myself to function.

The euthanasia proceeded quietly and efficiently. The bereavement process continued in expected fashion. I hugged each of the owners and expressed not only my sorrow at their loss, but my relief that they had each other to share the burden. They never knew that their remaining pet had used my doctor's bag as a "mosh pit," and they would never know the ridiculous movie poster that had flashed into my mind at the most sensitive moment.

How did I find myself building such a safety net of irreverent humor into my rational thought? How could I explain it? I was just the typical animal-loving teenager who fell in love with the idea of helping animals, alleviating their suffering and repairing their injuries. It had never occurred to me that the animals don't arrive on their own bearing little notes from home and their own plastic credit cards. I also spent no time dwelling on the reality of the loss that is an inevitable part of our lives with animals. When and how did this adaptation happen and what gives me these ideas? Humor is a universal antidote. I hope that it is in the best interest of all.

Looking back over more than thirty years of practice, I see myself as Vet Noir. I always tried to do the right thing, and I hope I usually did. Many times when my brain was totally in gear, my tongue was planted firmly in my cheek. The unseen machination of this serious profession is often quite funny.

CHAPTER 2
Dr. Fox

Sitting in the lecture hall wearing dark green barn coveralls seemed ridiculous at the time, but I wouldn't dare show up in any other attire. In front of the room was the mandatory expanse of a blank chalkboard, but I knew that I was about to experience the presence of a veterinary legend. I shivered with anticipation mixed with a little twinge of fear. This was not just another classroom; this was the domain of the great Dr. Francis Fox.

During the time that I attended Cornell Veterinary College, Dr. Fox was a force to be reckoned with. His credentials were extensive. He had pioneered the field of large animal veterinary care, and more specifically, bovine practice. He was widely published, authored many texts, and referenced by anyone who was involved in veterinary care of farm animals. He was a formidable presence, and he did not entertain fools lightly. Therein lay the dread that kept veterinary students awake at night.

To compare Dr. Fox's demeanor with another profession, one would have to conjure an image of a Marine drill sergeant on Parris Island dressed in green coveralls and barn boots but with slightly less tolerance for his uninformed newbies. His physical presence was intimidating; his keen stare could bore holes through any student trying to construct a tenuous diagnostic plan, and his silences were even more frightening than his verbal tirades. Before the era of political correctness, he could speak exactly what was on his mind and never give a thought to the sensitive inner psyche of his students.

We lived in fear of attending his class, and yet, like a good amusement park ride, we couldn't wait to sit down and experience the potential thrills and horror that were bound to occur. We would walk out the door of the classroom at the end of each lecture exhilarated to find that we were still intact bodily, able to walk and talk. (Actually, some students occasionally left minus the ability to speak, but invariably they returned to normal.) This was the thrill of victory or agony of defeat that made up Dr. Fox's Large Animal Medicine class.

The first two years of veterinary college were primarily devoted to classroom and laboratory subjects. We learned the machinations of our prospective patients on a microscopic and chemical level. Our major insight into the world we were about to enter was in Anatomy class where we tediously dissected the preserved cadavers that became our constant companions for many months. Then, like a moth emerging from a cocoon, we entered our junior year and a new world. Suddenly, we were faced with clinical classes dealing with real life cases and animals that retained the gift of life. It was heady stuff, and most of us suddenly realized that there was a light at the end of this tunnel. We allowed ourselves to dream of actually having that DVM attached to our names and that we would soon be stepping out into the world as bona fide veterinarians.

With two years of training under our belts, as unprepared as Christians driven into the coliseum, we marched off to Large Animal Medicine class and the infamous Dr. Fox. It was a glorious spectacle. He began with the assumption that we knew nothing of value and proceeded to try to salvage us as potential saviors of the nation's food animals. He cared not that few of us at that stage intended to become large animal practitioners. He turned up his nose at the thought of any of us considering wasting our time and valuable degree treating what he referred condescendingly to as "chi-hooa-hooas." This last statement was accompanied by a withering sneer of disdain as he spat the word off his tongue. In his world, there were two types of veterinarians—the real ones who treated farm animals, and the traitors posing as veterinarians who sidled into their cozy small animal clinics every morning and did what they tried to imagine was work. I must admit, that after being under his tutelage for my final two years, I was always able to spell Chihuahua without hesitation, although I can never do it without a frightening visual of the look on his face as he spat out the little dog's name. I am positive that if canvased as to our prospective career goals, one hundred per cent of my class would have sold their souls to the devil before they would have admitted to wanting to work on small animals.

Nobody slacked off in Dr. Fox's class. Not ever. He had a mother's instinct for knowing when plots were brewing or whispering was happening even if the whisper was quiet as a silent dog whistle. He had a horrible gift that allowed him to look at a face, usually from way across a lecture hall, and without uttering a word, he would know instantly if that individual was paying attention to the lecture and if he or she would be able to answer a question on the subject at hand. And God help that individual if he or she was found to be lacking. He would pounce, and before the interrogation was done, the student would be reduced to a blithering idiot before the class. He was scathing in his critiques, but he was always unbiased. Nobody escaped his winnowing fork.

During my schooling, women in the class were the minority. In fact, the ratio of men to women in my class was ten to one. There was always a concern in those early feminist years that the women would not receive fair or equal treatment. I must report that without fail, Dr. Fox took as much joy in putting the women through the gauntlet as he did the men. In his eyes, we were all equal as bottom-feeders in the food chain. But there was something different that I sensed early on and enjoyed to the utmost.

Although Dr. Fox would make grumpy complaints about "The Females," such as "The Females probably aren't going to like what I'm about to say," we remained nameless as an amorphous entity in his class. That was a blessing. I could see that he enjoyed it when one of us managed to outwit one of our male classmates. Despite his showy saber rattling, I was certain he hoped to see us succeed in a world of men.

Dr. Fox, beyond all else, expected us to use our heads and think logically, with or without the help of books. He posed questions in class of a highly practical nature that the textbooks did not specifically cover. He then frowned and stormed back and forth at the front of the lecture hall as gifted student after high achiever was unable to give the answer. All he asked was that we use all of our life experience and put it to use with our veterinary education. He would pick out a student and throw question after question at him, often leaving him insensible. When he started questioning the audience, I had found that the best tactic was to appear absorbed in note taking, head down, scribbling wildly in my notebook. If he could not make eye contact, he could not call on me because I was a nameless member of "The Females," and therefore, not identifiable as an individual. It was my protective coloration.

During one class, the lecture concerned a situation where horses ingest grain too quickly and a wad of it becomes lodged in their esophagus, preventing passage of food or water. This, in horseman's terms is called "choke," and is a miserable situation for doctor and patient. It usually requires extended ministration by the vet and can be life threatening. When a horse has choked once, it tends to happen again, especially if some scar tissue forms a slightly narrowed spot in the esophagus. This often happens to some valuable show horses and can be a big problem.

Dr. Fox questioned the class on what advice they could give the owner of such a horse to prevent the horse from gulping down large quantities of grain and choking again. Some brave soul raised his hand and offered the advice that the owner could hand-feed small amounts to the horse, little by little. Dr. Fox was enraged by the impracticality of this suggestion and moved on to another sacrificial lamb. The interrogation continued and the suggestions became more ludicrous.

During this time, I thought I knew the answer to his question. I had grown up with horses and one of mine had always wolfed down his grain ration. I had placed several large, smooth rocks in his grain bucket so that he could not physically grab a large mouthful of grain, but had to use his lips and carefully pick the feed from around the stones. It had worked well for me, but I figured this was too simple and obvious and I feared the Wrath of Fox. I remained silent.

The inquisition continued. Our professor would not quit until someone came up with the answer to his riddle. My heart pounded harder and harder. Student after student gave their proposals and all went down in the Flames of Fox. I finally couldn't stand it anymore and decided to join my fallen comrades.

I tentatively raised my hand, and to my horror, he pointed at me. In his nasal twang he drawled, "Yeeesss?"

I could feel my face flush scarlet and wasn't sure that I could even get the words out, but it was too late to go back.

"Put big rocks in the grain bucket so he can't get a large mouthful of grain?" I whispered.

"*What?*" he boomed.

I threw caution to the wind, took a deep breath, and blurted it out again, but this time much louder. The ensuing silence was physically painful for me.

"Now, see what you've done?" he roared from the lectern. "You've gone and let *The Female* show you up!"

Robin Truelove Stronk DVM

This was perhaps the sweetest, and to me, the most reassuring two sentences ever spoken. It was right on a par with hearing, "It's not cancer after all."

Stories of Dr. Fox were told throughout the school and we were all aware of his influence long before we reached his class in our junior year. During the summer between my sophomore and junior year, I had my first face-to-face encounter with him. I was employed in the Department of Reproductive Studies at the school. This, of course, was another one of my life ironies, as my maiden name, Truelove, lent itself to jokes and ribbing. I would like to say I enjoyed these moments, but I have to admit the entertainment soon faded, although I usually persevered with my best game face.

One of my supervisors was a wonderful professor named Dr. Hunt. He spent very little time in the laboratory and most of his time on the road visiting farms and collecting various samples. Although he was more than capable of doing his rounds alone, he would often invite me along, "to help out." I rarely felt that I added much by way of assistance on these outings but thoroughly enjoyed the respite from the laboratory and learned some valuable information. One piece of valuable information was where to find a little roadside diner that served fresh bear claw pastries on certain days of the week.

One morning, Dr. Hunt rushed into the lab and asked if I wanted to go out to one of the farms to see an unusual case. It was such a unique problem that none other than the great Dr. Fox was going to examine the cow. This verged on the historic for me. Without hesitation, I dropped what I was doing and went with Dr. Hunt. It was almost unheard of for a student to see Dr. Fox in action with a clinical case in the field.

As we took the elevator down to meet Dr. Fox, Dr. Hunt kindly filled me in on a few insider secrets. Dr. Fox was known to enjoy a chew of tobacco while working outside the school. On the occasion that he had a student in his vehicle, shortly after leaving the school he

13

would pull out his tobacco pouch, ceremoniously stuff a quid in his cheek, and then turn, and offer the pouch to the student. To turn him down was considered shameful and lacking fortitude. (Remember, this was another era.)

Then, as soon as the student put some of the tobacco in his cheek, Dr. Fox would announce that he had just one rule in his car. "No spitting unless the car is stopped at a stop sign." Driving the long miles between farms in upstate New York, there are no stop signs. He got fiendish delight watching the smug student turn shades of green. On occasion, he had to stop when the student begged for mercy and was sick next to the road.

After filling me in on this, Dr. Hunt said I could do whatever I wanted if the situation should arise, he just wanted me to be forewarned. I felt that I had just been handed the Rosetta Stone.

We met Dr. Fox. He stared impassively at me as Dr. Hunt introduced me. I think he managed a "Humph," but not much more. We got in his car, Dr. Hunt in the passenger's seat and me in the backseat. Sure enough, we were on the road only a short time when I saw him starting to sneak quick looks back at me as he pulled out his tobacco pouch and prepared his chew. As predicted, he reached over the seat with the open pouch angled at me and asked, "Chew?"

I had kept my face pleasantly blank up until this point. I flashed a smile and said, "Oh, thanks!"

I reached in, fished out a small pinch of dried leaves, rolled them between my fingers, and then went through the motions of tucking the wad into my mouth against my cheek. As I withdrew my fingers, I carefully palmed the leaves, slid my hand down out of sight, and deposited it down inside my barn boot. I pushed my cheek out slightly with my tongue and kept a satisfied smile on my face.

Now the real fun began. Poor Dr. Hunt had no idea what was going on and must have felt as if he had led me astray. Dr. Fox was settling in for grand drama on his way to the farm. I felt like a fox in a henhouse hoping I wouldn't be struck by lightning before I was able to enjoy the denouement of my little scheme.

Minutes ticked away as the professors made small talk about the upcoming case we would be examining. Dr. Fox had announced his One Rule of the Car and I had nodded in agreement. As we drove, I would let my attention drift and cast my glance out the side window. Every time that I did, I noticed Dr. Fox glancing up in his rearview mirror, waiting for the moment that I would cave in. Occasionally, I would move my tongue around as though moving the chew to a more comfortable location. The look of puzzlement on Dr. Hunt's face was making me pity that he was not in on my ruse. Time passed and we had been driving at least forty minutes. There was a palpable moment when I think Dr. Fox just gave up on his anticipated fun. I think I saw him shrug after the last time he checked on me in his rearview mirror. I beamed a friendly smile back at him and could barely contain threatened giggles.

We arrived at the farm, met the owner, and proceeded to our patient who was lying on the ground looking unwell. Dr. Fox turned to Dr. Hunt and asked, "Does 'The Female' know how to put a halter on a cow?"

Wordlessly, Dr. Hunt handed me the halter, and I put it on our patient. The examination progressed as Dr. Fox addressed all his conversation to Dr. Hunt or the cow's owner.

Occasionally a suggestion was made that "The Female" might want to look at some aspect of the cow's body or questions of what "The Female" might know. I took this to be his acquiescence for having his fun ruined, and yet giving me a nod for having stayed on my feet. Although this appears to be terribly demeaning in the telling, in truth, I felt that I had passed my first trial by fire. I will always remember the episode as The Day I Rode with Dr. Fox.

The culmination of our ordeal with Dr. Fox was his final examination. There was no predicting what form the exam might take.

Because he was dedicated to the learning process, every examination was unique and individual. There would be no reliance on old copies stored in some dusty files for prompts. Each examination was a new creation. When the time came, he announced that we would need to report for the process in groups of four, which had been assigned. We were to wear our coveralls and barn boots and bring our large animal thermometers and stethoscopes. There was an audible thump as sixty-six hearts fell to the floor. This was going to be a practical examination, not a traditional pen on paper affair. There would be no "do-overs," no going back to mull over a tough question. We would apparently be in a barn with our inquisitor and live animals asked to perform basic functions of a physical exam and to answer rapid-fire questions on the spot.

Dr. Fox considered the ability to do a good, thorough physical examination, the most basic qualification of a veterinarian. After thirty-five years of practice, I realize he was 100 percent correct. With no access to laboratory equipment, reference guides, or clinical aides, he expected us to use our eyes, hands, nose, and ears to examine our patient and bring forth pertinent information and observations. The only warning we received was that we had to be completely sure of the normal temperature, pulse, and respiration rates of all the usual farm animals. No cheat sheets and no variance; we needed to know these numbers cold.

To a man, or Female as the case may be, we pounced on this factoid as the key to the entire exam. For hours on end, we fired questions at one another: "Normal pulse range of a sheep … Normal temp range of a horse …." It was not enough to know that a cow with a temperature of 101degrees was normal; we needed to know that between 100 and 102 degrees was normal. As the frenzy built, our hysteria became monumental. We shared nightmares of being faced with an obese beef cow in the barn and having Dr. Fox demand that we take the animal's pulse and declare where it stood in the normal range. In retrospect, never have so many made so much uproar over so little.

Exam day came. We suited up, checked our large animal rectal thermometers for the thousandth time, and ensured that the loop on the end was securely attached to a safety cord and clip to attach to the beast's fur so that the instrument would not be "lost in action." We worried over our stethoscopes, idly scratching a finger over the diaphragm to check if it had mysteriously gone mute on us. Lists of numbers tumbled through our sleep-deprived minds, blurring species and swirling into nonsense. I joined the three classmates in my assigned group, and we marched with heads down, as if to slaughter, to the designated test site.

In my group were three other male members of the class. They were big stout farm boys who had grown up milking cows and had the wrists and forearms to testify to long hours of intense manual labor. All through the four years of veterinary school, we were often divided up alphabetically, and so the four of us had worked together frequently during the last three years. I knew they were experienced cow handlers and they would defer to me when we had horse problems to tackle. We went through the clinic to the designated test site and found nobody there to meet us. Instead, there was a note instructing us to report to Dr. Fox's office.

Confused, we reversed direction and wended our way back through the school to the hallowed hall of the great one's office. Most of us had never even been through the door before. We knocked and immediately heard the Yankee nasal retort, "Come in!" We jumped through the door as if we had received an electric shock. Inside was a line of four chairs. Dr. Fox was leaning comfortably in front of them on his desk. He instructed us to take seats. Now we were more disoriented than ever. Surely, he wasn't going to march a Holstein in here for our exam? The room was overheated and we quickly began to sweat in our coveralls and winter barn attire.

With no introduction, he began nodding at us in random order and firing questions. "What's the normal temperature of a goat?" he asked, pointing to one of my classmates.

I immediately began thinking ahead to what the next question might be, desperately reviewing temperatures of other species. My classmate answered, and not missing a beat, Dr. Fox swung around to the last person in line and queried, "Was that answer right?" Of course, none of us had paid attention to the classmate on the firing line; we were too busy worrying about what our question might be.

We became a study in "deer in the headlights" syndrome as Dr. Fox fired off questions in random order up and down the line, changing topics in a chaotic fashion and apparently having the time of his life. He would switch from questions of contagious diseases to normal pulse rates, to reportable diseases to location for auscultation of the rumen of a cow.

Good God, the man expected us to think on our feet! This was truly a mental gymnastic competition. There was no time to anticipate or allow one's mind to drift. We had to attend to every word of every person's answer. If a classmate's answer was sound and we relaxed, he may move on down the line and suddenly ask, "What more can you add to that?"

Sweat poured off our faces. A trip to the barn for a hands-on with a cow now seemed like a walk in the park.

At a point where we all felt thoroughly pummeled, the examination seemed to be winding down. We prayed for salvation for just a few more minutes and then it would be over. Still, there was no practical application for thermometer or stethoscope. It seemed that bit had been a diversion. Then, he pulled out his last trick. He walked up to one classmate, and as he nodded to the next in line, said, "Take his pulse." This was to demonstrate our expertise in finding and noting the pulse in any species, or so we thought.

The student fumbled around but eventually was able to report a pulse rate. Dr. Fox took the student's other wrist and rechecked. He scowled but didn't comment. He moved on to the next victim. Again, he was instructed to take the pulse of the next man in line.

This fellow, whose pulse was to be taken, was a big guy. He had arms and wrists of impressive girth. His classmate fumbled and his hands shook. He repositioned himself repeatedly but could not seem to find the appropriate spot to feel the pulse. Finally, Dr. Fox lost patience, he pointed to me (nameless Female) and said, "Oh, go ahead, take the Obese One's pulse."

There are pivotal moments in our lives when we make life-altering decisions with no real conscious thought. People jump off bridges with bungee cords tied to their feet or heroically lead a charge across a battlefield. There is no good explanation for what I did next and there certainly was no plan. I was seized by the moment. Without hesitation, I stepped forward, took Dr. Fox's wrist, and stared intently at my wristwatch.

I was not expelled from school. I actually passed the final exam. To my complete surprise I somehow ended up joining a mixed animal practice after graduation where I did primarily dairy cattle work. And, best of all, I had seen the great Dr. Fox smirk. It was the closest thing to a smile that I saw in four years.

CHAPTER 3
What's in a Name?

Every eye in the room was on me. Of this, I was acutely aware. I felt the heat surge up from my collar. I don't just blush, I erupt, and I was about to experience a record breaker.

After having spent the last three years of my life in a male-dominated environment, I seldom contemplated the ramifications of my gender minority. Our student group worked together as well as any large group of people subjected to daily stress and problems. The gender issue was, in my opinion, a nonissue. It was with this blissful blind spot that I had arrived in the laboratory for Reproductive Studies.

As a junior veterinary student, I had looked forward to this class. It covered the gamut from cows to pigs to dogs and cats. The bulk of the material related to large animals, but a few classes covered issues of small animals. The laboratory sessions that accompanied classroom material illustrated what we had been learning. In one laboratory session, we had observed a Cesarean section on a Beagle. The only other session dedicated to small animal reproduction involved a male dog. Today, we would learn to collect samples and evaluate them for use in artificial insemination. This sounded worthwhile to me as a potential small animal practitioner.

The professor arrived at the Reproductive Studies lab with a lively male Beagle. He explained the process of obtaining a sample and showed us the equipment we were to use. It sounded uncomplicated. We all moved into a circle around the professor and our candidate for collection.

I was the lone female member of this group. I suddenly noticed that twenty-one male students and I would share this indelicate display. I decided to shake off the concern, as we were all adults and our goal here was knowledge. I would do my best to fade into the background with the guys and hope for the best. I made a mental note to avoid any fits of coughing, dropping of writing materials, or certainly, any posing of unnecessary questions.

The collection process went as promised. The professor manually stimulated the dog to produce his sample into a ridiculous looking latex apparatus called an artificial vagina. It was apparent that this particular dog was no stranger to the device. There was no beauty required for the eye of this beholder. He went right to business to "git 'er done," and he did. All this transpired with very little comment from the assembled group. Apparently, I was not the only one feeling a bit ill at ease.

We then analyzed the sample microscopically, and I felt we had received a thorough demonstration of the basics for our small animal veterinary practice. I was relieved that everyone had shown maturity and diplomacy. I was even glad that our subject looked none the worse for wear. It was another good day with no complications, or so I thought.

The professor gathered us back together with the Beagle and announced, "I'd like one of you students to collect this dog again to demonstrate for the class so we can be sure that you have learned the technique."

Without hesitation, twenty-one pairs of eyes swung around and settled on me. Twenty-one pairs of eyes, all sporting both X and Y-chromosomes. Some perverted mental process known only to the male of the species had chosen the sacrificial subject. The fact that my last name was Truelove only added to the bacchanal atmosphere. I began some lightning fast deductions.

Although our Beagle was enthusiastic and well versed in his craft, it had been less than an hour since his first performance. What were the chances he could return to the stage like some seasoned porn star and recreate the first show? It was bound to be a more arduous task requiring more time and effort. What about the possible outcomes? I saw there were only two possibilities. If I could entice the dog to comply, I would be the subject of derision and suggestive asides from my classmates for months afterward. On the other hand, if I failed at my task, I would be the subject of derision and suggestive asides from my classmates for months afterward. My analysis complete, I realized this was an example of the dreaded "no-win" situation. My plan of action was clear.

I feel it is of utmost importance to pick your battles wisely. I realized that surrender and beating a hasty retreat was in the best interest of my army of one. I stepped forward, apologized to the professor, and announced that I was, "Damned if I do and damned if I don't, and I will now be retiring to the women's locker room to review my notes." And I turned and left the lab.

In truth, the woman's locker room during that time was the secretary's locker room. There were too few women students in the school to warrant a separate locker room. So I escaped to a refuge where the women met to eat their lunches and talk about female issues. I sighed deeply and renewed myself in its nurturing atmosphere. There would be other days and other conflicts, but I had extricated myself from this one unscathed.

***

I had not considered the possibility that my quest for bovine vaginal mucus could become a religious crusade. Sitting on a bundle of newspapers jammed into the back of a Volkswagen Beetle, I realized that was exactly what was happening.

Working in the Department of Reproductive Studies during the summer between my junior and senior years had been an excellent learning experience. Besides assisting various researchers in the laboratory, I was expected to work on a project of my own. With the guidance of my supervising professor, I had chosen to evaluate whether an antisperm antibody in cows caused infertility. It was a good project; it had some obvious immediate merit in the field, was of a practical nature, presented an uncomplicated protocol, and best of all, afforded me many opportunities to get outside in the open air. Every hour spent outside the lab was a glorious interlude as far as I was concerned. I was much happier climbing over fences and handling cows than wearing a white coat and balancing industrial-sized centrifuges.

I reached a point in my research where it became essential to have samples of vaginal mucus from cows in heat. I needed many samples, the more the better. The value of my findings balanced on the number of subjects included in the study. The veterinary school had several milking dairy herds, and as part of my job, I had been inseminating the cows that came into heat. I would collect a sample for my research before inseminating each potential mother. This was good to a point, but it did not afford me with the number of samples I needed. The issue boiled down to how I could find and have access to a large number of dairy cows at the perfect moment of their reproductive cycle and collect samples from them.

My supervisor came up with the solution. I would accompany a local artificial inseminator on his rounds and collect samples from the cows before he made his deposit. I loved this option, not only because it would provide many samples for my research, but also because it would get me out of the lab for an entire day.

After being given a name and phone number, and told that the party to whom I would be speaking was a wonderful person and would be a great asset to my inquiry, I called and set up an appointment to spend a day on the road with the inseminator.

My day of fieldwork had started early. As instructed, I met my mentor at his home at 6:00 AM. Dairy farmers awake long before sunrise, and they expect anyone who works with them to do the same. I had directions to the home and found the address with no problem. The inseminator invited me into his house and introduced me to his wife. They offered me a cup of coffee, and I sat down at their kitchen table. I had expected to be off on the road in no time, but that was not to be.

While sitting with our coffee, Mr. and Mrs. Inseminator seemed in no rush. They asked about my schooling and quickly moved on to inquiries about my personal life. Was I married? What was my family life like? Soon, they swept into the topic of religion. This was a little strange considering I was sitting at the table of complete strangers at a very early morning hour, drinking coffee, expecting to go out to meet a bevy of hormonally charged bovines.

The couple was bold in their questioning, and feeling quite beholden to them, I felt compelled to fill them in on the paltry details of my religious upbringing and beliefs. It became apparent to me, even though I truly was a babe in the religious woods, that they had strong fundamentalist foundations. In fact, they were on a mission to enlist every lost soul they met. Unfortunately, this included misdirected veterinary students who only came in search of the rather dubious commodity called bovine vaginal mucus. I had not realized that bartering for my soul might be part of this deal.

I'm sure that their motives were honorable if, in my case, misdirected. I do not remember what I may have said to satisfy them, although I am positive that I neither converted nor claimed rebirth of any sort. Eventually, as the sun rose higher and higher in the sky, we collected our belongings and headed out on our rounds.

Being used to the "vet-mobiles" for transportation and equipment storage at the veterinary school, I expected a vehicle of some magnitude to ride in on our appointed calls. To my dismay, I was ushered to a Volkswagen Beetle. Peering inside, I saw that it held only one seat, and that of course was for the driver. The space for the passenger seat was occupied by a large, cylindrical liquid nitrogen tank that held the precious insemination samples. The container looked like R2D2 sitting patiently waiting for his next mission. The back seat was gone. That space was filled with the accumulated detritus of years of travel and work. An anthropologist would have had a field day in that area behind the driver's seat. Papers, remnants of lunches, bottles, notices, winter vests, old boots and gloves, and insemination pipettes strewn in a chaotic orgy.

My new friend, or savior, as he may have seen himself, did not indicate where I might ensconce myself for our day's journey. I opened the door and attempted to sweep some debris aside to find an area big enough to plant my bottom. He looked back, shrugged, grabbed a bound bundle of newspaper, and plopped it into the cleared area. Obviously, he was more concerned about the fate of my soul than he was about my creature comforts.

As we drove along, I resolved to be as unobtrusive as possible. I certainly did not want to create any extra work for my patron. At the farms, he would introduce me and give me a head start to the indicated cows so I could get my samples before he inseminated each of them. This was straightforward, and I expected that I'd stay out of everyone's way.

To collect my samples, I needed to pass a long pipette, virtually identical to those used by the inseminator, but instead of depositing a sample, I would attach a syringe and apply suction and obtain a small sample of the mucus pooled on the floor of the cow's vagina. I then placed the sample (a viscous material that did not lend itself to tidy pouring or measurement) into plastic vials labeled with the cow's identification number and date. Later in the lab, I would assay these samples for the presence of an antibody directed against bovine sperm.

As a species, cows are generally docile, especially dairy cows. They are a congenial lot and used to being handled. Most of the farms we visited had cows in stanchions that loosely restrained them, preventing them from backing up and turning around. Other barns were free-stall barns, meaning that the cows could lounge around as they pleased. There were stalls with low partitions where the cows would go whenever they wanted to lie down to rest and chew their cuds. All the cows were identified with bright plastic ear tags bearing their unique number.

We had a routine of driving to farms and making introductions and explanations to the owners. We would receive our list of ear tag numbers, and the farmer would accompany us to chat with the inseminator and oversee the work. I would move off as quickly as possible and begin collecting my samples. Again, I allowed myself to be lulled into thinking the day would go great, and I would return to the lab with a treasure trove of samples.

Partway through the morning, we entered a free-stall barn and went through the usual drill. The owner was very curious about my needs and asked many questions about the premise. He would scratch his head, tilt his cap back on his forehead (a sure indication of deep thought in a farmer, I had found), and peer down his nose at me. He really wanted to understand the whole procedure before we got underway. I tried to be patient and helpful, but I could see the inseminator glancing at his wristwatch, and I knew that I was putting him behind schedule. Finally I seemed to have satisfied his inquiries and I sped away to look for my subject, number 49.

I found good old number 49 hanging out in a stall facing the road.

She turned her head lazily to have a look at me as I approached and then went back to her bovine ruminations. I quickly prepared the pipette, syringe, and a ready collection tube. Unfortunately, I found that this candidate had not read Miss Elsie the Cow's Book of Bovine Manners. When cows are in heat, they are cooperative, even receptive to any attention that involves their more delicate female appurtenances. Number 49 shifted and danced, hopped from one hind foot to the other, and moved in ways that made it impossible for me to pass the pipette.

I tried to keep one of my shoulders against her hindquarters knowing that if I allowed her a bit of room she could turn and exit the stall. I doubted that I would be able to corral her again alone. I did not intend to disturb the men to ask for assistance. They were at the other side of the barn, deep in conversation, and oblivious to my plight. Of course, I could have chosen to pass by number 49 and leave her forever out of my bovine research, but I was ever tenacious, and wasn't about to fold yet.

My attempts became more hurried, and number 49's resistance increased in amperage. She would now let out a disconcerting bellow at odd intervals. I was actually contemplating abandoning my effort when number 49 put a halt to the proceedings. Without warning, she leaned back against me, gave a tremendous lunge forward, and propelled herself out the window of the barn. This may sound impossible, but indeed, it did happen. The windows in free-stall barns are large and wide to allow maximum passage of air. It was summer and so the windows were all open. Although it was a bit of a tight fit, my subject made it through in one leap up to the point of her delicate pendulous udder. This hung her up for a moment, head and shoulders free, and hindquarters dangling in the window. We never give cows, especially dairy cows, credit for athleticism, but this was a remarkable show. She gave one more lunge and was out the window.

In the ensuing silence, my heart threatened to stop. I expected to look out the window and see this valuable animal crumpled in a pile, at least one of her legs broken. At the very least, I felt sure that she must have terminally damaged her udder, rendering her useless on this farm. I looked for blood trails but saw none.

At this point, the owner and the inseminator arrived at my side having sprinted across the barn. The look on their faces spoke volumes, but the inseminator did manage to sputter, "What did you *do?*"

Words failed me, and I turned away just in time to see my bovine hurdler blissfully trotting down the road, leaving the premises, unmarred udder swaying merrily with every step. Her ears were up and she looked like a child running off to the playground. Relieved, I just looked back at them and said, "Right … well, I guess I'll go catch the cow if you can give me a halter."

Catching the cow managed to fill the rest of our time at the farm. This was fine with me. There was no way that I would attempt to take samples from any more of this man's herd. As I dived into the back of the Beetle and scurried to my roost on the newspapers, I could feel his steely gaze boring a hole in me. I also noted his cap was pushed *way* back on his head.

CHAPTER 4
Hats off to the Ladies

I studied my image in the woman's room mirror and adjusted my hat to perfection. The first day of senior year was going to be really special. We all had our fill of classroom and laboratory. We wanted to be out on the playing field. Put me in coach, I'm ready to play. Or so we had thought. The ambulatory clinic was my assignment for this first rotation. My roommate and I had chosen to be partners for our first clinic round. Partnered with a senior clinician, we would be on the road all day visiting farms and stables doing veterinary work. We could apply our knowledge and see the local sites.

One tradition among Cornell veterinary students called for us to wear a unique or quirky hat on ambulatory rounds. To show up wearing a baseball cap was bland and uncaring. A lot of thought went into the choice of an ambulatory hat. It would be our signature for the entire senior year. I'm sure the farmers were less than charmed, if they even noticed our eclectic headwear, so it probably only served as entertainment for our classmates. I thought I had found the ideal chapeau—a red engineer's cap with white polka dots.

My roommate and I arrived for the first day of clinics resplendent in our dark green coveralls, tall rubber barn boots, and goofy hats. There were high spirits among the students as we took photos and kidded around while loading our various vehicles and preparing for a day of excitement. As usual, I anticipated a smooth day with no hitches. As usual, I was very wrong.

The clinician assigned to us probably had drawn the short straw. If he needed to rely on assistants with years of large animal background, we weren't the ones. If he needed brawny helpers to muscle some obstinate beef cow, he was also going to be disappointed. But we made up for any deficit in these departments with our ebullient attitudes and occasional home baked goods we brought along. We felt very lucky to have been assigned to this clinician. He had one of the best natures of any of the professors in the large animal clinic. He was a great teacher and was patient to a fault. He was a big tall fellow and his quiet ways soothed man and beast alike. We were sure he was a wonderful role model and soon found that we were right. We would be riding on calls with him for a week.

The day was ideal. Early autumn in upstate New York is inspiring. As we drove, our professor filled us in on some of the tasks we would face on our first call. It was a medium-sized dairy farm and there were quite a few jobs to be done. Some cows needed pregnancy checks, small calves needed vaccinations, a cow had a sore foot that would need examining, and one cow was off its feed and seemed sick. We would be seeing a whole gamut of health care in one visit, which was just what we wanted to experience in the real world. What a perfect day!

We arrived and the farmer reviewed what needed to be done. He oriented us as to which animals were to be found in which barns. We started with the pregnancy checks. Our instructor would lean on the cow, have one of us perform the pregnancy check by rectal palpation, and then he would repeat the process to check on our findings. We found we were doing quite well. With few exceptions, my partner and I were both making accurate diagnoses. We began to feel like a team.

Quite soon, we imagined smoothly introducing ourselves as "Doctor." We started to exude confidence.

Having ascertained that we both had basic cow knowledge, the instructor decided to split us up. He sent my roommate to a nearby barn that housed the calves. He provided her with the vaccine, gave a few words of instruction, and sent her off. He sent me to the barn that housed the sick cow. I was to give her a thorough physical examination and make a tentative diagnosis and treatment plan. Our teacher would be examining the cow with the bad foot, and as soon as he was done, he would come and check on my findings. I strutted off to meet my first legitimate large animal patient.

The cow was in a tie stall at the end of an aisle. She wore a halter with a lead rope attached. The rope was tied to the front end of the wooden stall. The stall rose slightly above my hip. The cow was obviously sick. There was no shine to her eyes, and she stood with her back arched as though she were quite uncomfortable. My mind raced with possibilities. She was a young heifer and had been out on green grass. A quantity of semi-liquid bright green manure under her in the stall indicated that she wasn't suffering from any kind of intestinal obstruction. Green grass is a laxative, so this type of manure was typical in this situation.

I continued my observations and took her rectal temperature. The next helpful piece of information was to check on the motility of the cow's gut. A healthy cow experiences large waves of contractions across its rumen that occur several times a minute. By placing the head of the stethoscope in the hollow of the left flank, these drawn out rumbling noises sound almost like a distant storm. To reach the necessary spot, I had to squeeze in between the cow and the partial wall of the stall. For reasons I still do not understand, this ended up being a very big mistake.

Without warning, the cow began to kick violently at me. Cows do not kick backward like a horse. They kick with one leg at a time, scooping it forward, almost as far as their head on occasion and slamming it back. She had me pinned between her and the wall, and in rapid-fire succession, she nailed me. The cow's hoof looks innocuous, but when applied in this manner, the claws are very sharp and very, very hard. I am not sure exactly how many times I was kicked, but I do know that I became immobilized and couldn't see any way out of the situation. If I moved forward toward her head, I would receive the end of her swinging hoof; moving back put me directly in the initial swing. I wasn't really thinking much, but my survival alarms were going off. Before I could make any decisions, a miracle happened.

I was suddenly lifted off my feet and swung through the air over the top of the stall wall. It was like a dream, but as my feet touched down again, I realized there were hands under my arms supporting me. My guardian angel was our intrepid clinician. His timing could not have been much better. He saw my plight, reached in, and plucked me out. He was a real barnyard hero.

Once I was in the safe zone, I became acutely aware of the pain that went along with my encounter. The cow's hoof had raked me up the inside of one thigh, across some very tender parts and back down the inside of the other thigh. I would later look back and wonder if a male of my height would have survived the attack. It was very clear from the liberal plastering of fresh green manure on my coveralls where I had been struck. Tears welled up in my eyes and I fought mightily not to cry.

My instructor scanned the area of damage, took a quick look at my face, and said the most humane thing that he could think of. "Why don't you just go take a little walk over there behind the barn?"

Thankfully, I hobbled off to vent my emotions alone. I dreaded the time of reckoning when I got home, removed my coveralls, and surveyed the damage.

When I had regained my composure, I returned to the main barn to find my group. Gently, I had tried to scrape the manure from my coveralls, but there was no hiding the fact that I looked like I had been sumo wrestling with a bovine. I heard voices approaching and recognized our clinician's voice. He came around the corner shaking his head from side to side and looking very puzzled. He told me that my roommate had been kicked in the shin by one of the calves while she was administering a vaccine and she, too had "gone for a little walk." I now recognized his euphemism for having a good cry. At this point, I actually felt more compassion for this saint of a man than I did for either of us wounded students.

Finally, reunited in the vet-mobile, we had very little to say. My roommate gingerly rolled up her pant leg to reveal a lump on her shin the size of an egg that was growing a deeper shade of purple by the minute. I chose to keep my battle wounds to myself. We did hear a few asides from our instructor about his inability to understand what happened to us. He had never had two students go down at the same call. He had never even had two wounded on the same day. I could see him looking at us as if he were afraid to take us anywhere. I had the distinct impression we would be doing a lot of observing for the next week. I imagined him conjuring us wrapped in survival suits and never letting us out of the vehicle.

That night, my roommate and I decided we needed a plan or we were never going to see action for the next week. If the clinician thought we were helpless wimps, he was not going to let us do anything. We decided humor was the best way to shake off the incident. Humor and a whole load of aspirin with some ice packs thrown in during the evening.

The next morning, I again surveyed my countenance in the bathroom mirror and this time I saw reality. Looking back at me from under that silly headgear was not a senior veterinary student but something more like a rodeo clown. I had a lot of ground to regain in the respect department.

Fortified with over-the-counter pharmaceuticals, we were able to hobble reasonably well. We showed up at the clinic early so that we could have our teacher's vehicle loaded and ready before he even arrived. When he made his appearance, he just stared at us. I imagined that he had dreamed all night that we might give him a break and not show up. He didn't look disappointed, but he certainly didn't look overly enthusiastic. He sighed and asked if we were ready for another day.

"Absolutely!" we replied, and then informed him that we had prepared properly for a day of farm calls with him. With that statement, we both spun around and showed him our backs where we had neatly pinned signs that read, "KICK ME."

CHAPTER 5
Wardrobe Malfunction

I wrestled valiantly with the monkey. He was much stronger than I would ever have guessed. Together we staggered back and forth before the door, but his simian power was undeniable. My attempts to calm him with kind words were lost over the cacophony of shrieking canines. Despite my best efforts, I was losing the battle as well as my pants.

Veterinarians are supposed to be professional people. They are expected to have control of their daily life and their clinics. People look up to them. In my senior year, I was only months away from graduation, and yet I was reduced to a red-faced, bumbling idiot before an entire crowd of pet owners. During my rotation through the small animal clinic, I had been assigned to an unusual case. Working in a referral and teaching hospital, we often saw strange diseases and exotic animals. Such was the case with this Woolly Monkey that had come under my care. The owner was a teenage girl hospitalized with an undiagnosed illness. Since monkeys are so close to humans in the evolutionary chain, they can transmit more diseases to humans than many other animals we keep as pets. Some of these, such as the B virus, have little effect on the monkey but can be devastating, even fatal, if contracted by a human being.

I had not much experience with monkeys. I had worked one summer in a pet shop that had a Capuchin monkey. It was quite tame and rode around on our shoulders. It had absolutely no manners, and when it saw a person in the store it found objectionable, it would revert from its mild-mannered state to screaming and pointing, jumping up and down on my shoulder. The thrill of being seen with a monkey on my shoulder soon paled due to these unpredictable outbursts. As a result, the monkey spent her days primarily confined to her cage.

This Wooly Monkey was bigger than the Capuchin and I was wary of him at first, especially concerned that he might be harboring a transmissible disease. But the monkey had been in the clinic for several weeks and was an exemplary patient. All of its blood tests had been taken and repeated a second time to ensure there was no danger in sending him home.

All during his stay, he had been kept in an isolation ward tucked away from the mainstream of activity, quite remote and very quiet. I had grown comfortable checking him twice daily and even thought he enjoyed my company. I did feel sorry for him since he was obviously a social animal, and I felt that he must be incredibly bored. Nobody even brought him a magazine.

When the day came for his release, I was delighted to be the one to spring him from his solitude. I had not met his owner yet, and I was sure she would be delighted to reunite with her pet.

The small animal clinic was a large and very busy place. It was well designed to ensure a smooth flow of traffic in the waiting room area. The seats and benches were arranged in a large semicircle at the entrance that faced the glassed-in reception desk and counters. A door to the left of the reception area led to the examination rooms. A door to the right of the reception area led from the examination rooms and hospital wards. The two doors only opened in one direction to ensure that traffic would move with the pattern and there would be no unexpected confrontations between dogs entering and exiting. It worked well.

I went to gather my charge from the isolation ward and began the long walk to the reception area where the owner would collect her pet. She was receiving all the discharge information in the professor's office, and as the monkey was entirely healthy, I was to meet her in the waiting room to transfer her pet. I wondered how a happy monkey met his owner. I was used to dogs leaping and barking and was anxious to see what the monkey version of this might be.

As this was a moderately large monkey, and he was comfortable walking next to me, I held his hand and allowed him to walk with me as a toddler would. I had moved him around this way before and thought it was very cute. We reached the door that entered the huge waiting room area. I swung the door open, turned to urge him through, and let the door swing shut behind us. Then chaos erupted.

I had never stopped to think that the average American house pet has never seen a monkey. Every dog in the waiting room sprang to voice and action. A mad chorus of barks, yelps, and screeches broke out. Dogs dived off their owners' laps, bolted to the ends of their leashes, leaped into the air on their hind legs. If any of those dogs were there because they were sick, it certainly wasn't apparent at that point. But if I was taken aback, imagine the reaction of the poor monkey.

After spending weeks in abject silence, seeing only one human at a time and then only for a short period—certainly not ever seeing or hearing a dog—this poor monkey was terrified. He quickly chose me as the only source of possible salvation, lunged for my leg, and tried to climb up my body. This was a reasonable thing for the monkey to do. Unfortunately, it was a catastrophic event for me.

I was wearing the standard uniform issued by the vet school. In that less-than-equal time, there were distinct men's and women's uniforms. I had never liked the elastic waistband of the women's uniform pants and now I knew why. As the monkey clung and pulled, my trousers began to slide down over my hips. I did not dare let go of the monkey's hand, ever responsible to my duties. I tried without much success to preserve my dignity with my one free hand.

As the noise level rose, the monkey became more frantic. One side of my pants was down to my knees and the other side was following quickly. The laughter from the crowd in the waiting room was now getting louder than the barking. Nobody rushed to my aid. Not a Crocodile Hunter or Tarzan around.

There was no place to go. I had already administered a few quick hip checks to the door from which I had emerged, but it only opened one way. I would have to sprint the width of the room to get out of sight of the dogs and their owners. I scooped up the monkey with one arm, deposited him on my hip, grabbed what I could of the wayward pants with the other hand, and charged across the waiting room with the pants somewhere between my waist and knees.

Everything was in slow motion. I can still visualize some of the merry faces in the crowd. When I finally burst through the door that led back into the exam rooms, I put down the monkey, pulled up my pants, and found another senior student. I told him I had an "emergency" (indeed!) and asked if he would return the monkey to its owner. I'm sure he thought I was ill because of my flushed face and the fact that I could hardly speak. He willingly took the animal.

I never found out how the reunion went, but I wasn't worried about my replacement. The men's uniforms had proper waistbands with button and zipper. My classmate was safe.

CHAPTER 6
When Pigs Fly

Strangely, I could not erase the image of Arnold the pig in the television show *Green Acres* from my mind as I charged across the floor. My heart pounded; my lungs would not take in enough air for the task. Possibly, my deep enjoyment of bacon and pork chops had given me bad karma. Now the situation reversed and I was the potential food item.

My first encounter with pigs occurred during my senior year in veterinary school. One of the four clinical rotations was the ambulatory clinic where we assisted various large animal clinicians on their rounds to area farms. This included many dairy farms, large and small; riding stables and backyard horse establishments; veal operations; sheep farms, and even the occasional pig farm.

We were told to pick a partner from our class for this rotation, as we would be traveling in pairs. My roommate was from Long Island and had no background with any large animals. I had ridden horses most of my life, but I knew nothing practical about other large animal species. With the wisdom of youth, we felt we would be an ideal pair to travel the ambulatory route together. At least we knew we would get along with each other on the long drives between farms. The ambulatory clinicians had their work cut out for them.

We left on a cold winter day to visit a large pig farm located some distance from the college. On the drive, our instructor filled us in on our responsibilities. The tasks all sounded mundane and uncomplicated. We began to feel quite smug. One of the brood sows had given birth and we needed to give the piglets iron injections.

From our classroom lectures, we knew that baby pigs are born iron deficient. If not given a source of iron in their first few weeks of life, they become severely anemic and die. The pig's usual source of iron is from rooting in the dirt, but most pigs are kept on a concrete floor for ease of cleaning. Many old farmers would put a few shovels of dirt in the pig's pen when the piglets were a few days old so that they could root and ingest the iron themselves. But this is rather haphazard for a large-scale operation, so the injections ensure that each piglet gets as much iron as necessary.

We smiled and chatted about how cute the little newborns would be. We reviewed the anatomic landmarks we needed to know before injecting their little bodies. This sounded easy and we were looking forward to seeing our patients. The other major project on this farm was to vaccinate part of the herd. This would be a group of partially grown "feeder pigs," which were in the process of being raised for market. Our professor didn't have much to say about this task, but repeated several times that it was important to "stay on your feet." This was ambiguous but didn't sound very hard. I imagined small pigs bumping into my legs or being caught underfoot. No problem there.

We arrived at the farm and the owner led us out to the barn where the sows gave birth. Inside, we found a large area cordoned off with two strands of electric fencing. At the far corner was a large metal hood hanging down a few feet off the floor. It held a heat lamp. The sow and piglets lay quietly under the hood, the brood nursing, and the mother snorting and grunting occasionally. It was a serene and cozy scene.

However, mother pigs, especially those with newborns, are incredibly protective. They can shame an enraged pit bull. They don't ask questions and they take no prisoners. If there is any indication that one of her babies may be in trouble or taken from her, she will fight to the death. We needed to get the mother out from under the hood in order to treat the piglets. As owner and clinician discussed the possibilities, mother pig was getting suspicious. She rose and began a series of sharp barks. We could see her canine teeth. They were huge and sharp. The pig herself was enormous. She began to move around her litter, always keeping her massive body between them and us.

Immediately assessing our potential as being limited with nothing more than a glance, the owner and his assistant decided that, along with the clinician, they would go into the pen with a large sheet of plywood in front of them. They would try to corral the pig in a corner and hold her there by leaning on the plywood. This sounded like an excellent plan to my roommate and me as we stood in the safe zone outside the electric fence. We liked to think we were in a special category of feminists. We deemed ourselves practical feminists, which meant that in times of peril, survival comes first and idealism comes second. Then we realized that left the two of us to inject the piglets. Still, this was clearly the safer place to be, and the piglets were so small they would surely be easy to handle. Or so we thought.

Everyone stepped gingerly over the electrified fence. The taller men cleared it fairly easily, but my roommate and I just made it over by stretching and standing on our toes. Now the enraged mother pig started forward to do battle. This was good since it allowed the two men to move in and push her away from the piglets and into the corner. Her shrieks and squeals were the most ungodly sound I had ever heard. They were deafening. She threw herself against the plywood, determined to break through.

"Get those piglets done. *Fast!*" gasped our clinician as he strained to hold the partition in place.

We sprang into action, drew up the injections, and decided one of us would lie on her stomach to retrieve piglets from under the hood and hand them out; the other would give the injection. It was a good plan until the first piglet felt the touch of human hands and definitely didn't like it. Pain was not an issue to these little guys. They did not want to be touched by anything that was "not Mama." Screams that seemed impossible to be generated by something so small echoed through the barn. The mother pig's rage escalated. The men were having a very hard time restraining her. One of them yelled, "Hurry!"

Our part of the task seemed to go in slow motion. Tiny pigs proved difficult to hold as they squirmed and twisted in our grasp. Forgotten were our carefully reviewed anatomical landmarks. As long as the injection went into the pig somewhere, it was good. There were probably twelve piglets, but it seemed like twelve dozen as it became more obvious that we had only a few more seconds until Mama burst out.

Just as the last piglet got its shot, one of the men shouted, "*Run!*" as the porcine torpedo hit the plywood for the last time and blew past it.

It was winter and we were dressed for the cold. Each of us wore several layers of flannel, quilted vest, long underwear, and turtleneck shirt under our coveralls. Thick wool ski caps covered our heads. We had sturdy work boots on covered with black rubber barn boots that extended up to our knees. Despite our attire and complete lack of training, both my roommate and I sprinted across the length of that pen, and without breaking stride, easily cleared the electric fence with the mother pig's snout inches from our heels.

Neither one of us remembered any details from the moment we sprang to our feet until we landed outside the fence. Looking back, we could not believe either of us could clear a hurdle that high. My only regret is that we had no photographer on hand to document each of us, looking like the Michelin Man, clearing the hurdle, side-by-side, leading leg straight out, faces forward showing perfect Olympic style.

Once we had all caught our breath and our racing hearts were under control, we moved on to the next task. Neither the professor nor the pig farmer was looking very enthusiastic about the current staffing situation. Their expression could best be described as resigned. Regardless, we were sure we could redeem ourselves with the next assignment and prove our value in the large animal field.

We helped the professor prepare the vaccinations. On a large scale like this, the vaccine is loaded into a gun that looks something like a caulking gun. The point is placed against the animal, the trigger is squeezed, and it injects the unit of vaccine. This looked foolproof. The professor handed each of us a vaccine gun and he took one himself. He started to climb a fence into a maze of large pens. He looked back, studied us a moment and said, "Remember, stay on your feet."

We realized the implication of this comment as we climbed the fence, looked down, and saw our targets. They were big pigs. Actually, they looked like huge, long-legged racehorse pigs, not like the fat sedate barnyard creatures in children's books. The tops of their backs were just below our hips. They were narrow in the body, as they were growing and not fattened up yet. We watched as our professor waded into them. The pigs were not aggressive but seemed upset by the presence of humans in the pen. They began to mill about, shoving and pushing one another. As they passed by him, our professor nonchalantly placed the gun against the back of their neck, pulled the trigger, and injected the vaccine. He quickly marked them on the back with a piece of chalk to indicate an injected pig and he moved on.

My roommate and I grimly climbed down the fence. As we got closer to the ground, the pigs got bigger and taller. I finally started moving among them and managed to vaccinate a few. The "staying on your feet" part was exceedingly difficult. If I were in the way, the pigs would butt into me and didn't hesitate to try to mow me down.

I watched, fascinated as one of the pigs managed to charge at our professor while his legs were slightly parted. The pig passed between his legs and kept moving. The man was well over six feet tall, and I realized if one of these monsters tried that with me, I was going to be off my feet and on one wild ride. I began to take tiny mincing steps, trying to keep my legs together at all times. I stole a quick glance at my roommate and was amused to see she had come to the same conclusion. And so we did our own version of the City Slicker Two Step as we inched through the pens full of pigs administering vaccine at a very awkward pace. We did stay on our feet, and wondered on the long trip back to school if any previous student had ever been so unfortunate as to do otherwise.

***

It was early summer, a time when black flies swarm in the Northeast. The bite of these gnats packs a wallop. The initial bite usually goes unnoticed but produces a nasty swelling and an itch afterward. The flies have an affinity for biting certain parts of the anatomy, the eyelids being one of those areas. When a black fly bites an eyelid it swells and swells and can even swell the eye shut. In my case, it often did. Unfortunately, the afternoon before a certain pig came into my life; I had been working outdoors and had received a black fly sting on the edge of my upper eyelid.

The pig had been straining in labor for sometime and had not delivered a single piglet. I got directions to the farm and assured the owner that I would be right out. At the time of the call, I was struggling to see anything out of that swollen eye. Worse yet, the swelling gave me an odd drunken look that was not bound to inspire confidence in my new client. I gathered up the required equipment, reviewed dosages of various drugs that might be required for a birthing pig, and prepared to leave.

At the time, we had a pre-veterinary student working with us named Dave. He currently attended a school in the Midwest. He was a quiet fellow and always gave the impression that he had been born a century or more after his designated time. He was polite and soft-spoken but seemed perplexed by some of the slang or casual activities of daily life in a veterinary practice. He was a "marching to his own drummer" kind of a guy in my book. When I had appeared at the practice that morning, I saw the look of horror on his face when he saw my eye. I quickly explained what had happened lest he think I was the victim of domestic violence. Raised in the city where black flies dare not go, he looked somewhat relieved but a little incredulous. He seemed pleased to hear about our next patient and climbed into the practice truck with me.

The address I had been given was a neighborhood of closely placed modest homes. I wondered if I had misinterpreted the directions, but when we arrived, the owners appeared and seemed relieved to see me. Apparently, this was the correct place. Nobody seemed to notice my Cyclops-like appearance, and the owners quickly led us behind the house into a wooded area. Before our eyes (or my one good eye as was the case), was a veritable pig shantytown. A ramshackle conglomerate of wood, doors, old tires, and partitions all wired together formed several enclosures, each housing a large pig. It was a staggering scene, certainly nothing I would expect in this little neighborhood. The owners informed us that they had been raising a few pigs for some time and made a small profit selling them. Although I wondered what the local zoning board would have to say about this arrangement, it seemed to be an ambitious project and I applauded their creativity.

We looked over the haphazard enclosure and saw our patient. A huge sow was ensconced in a three-sided hut. The entire pig area was a sea of soft mud. No iron shots for these babies, they had the real thing. The pig was indeed laboring heavily with no result. My heart sank as I contemplated the possibility of a Cesarean section. My concerns were numerous: the area was the most unhygienic that I had encountered in a long time, I had no skilled assistant, I had not brought adequate surgical supplies, and worst of all, I had never performed or even seen a pig Cesarean section. I prayed for guidance. From my experience with pigs, I was even hesitant to climb in with this patient. The owners looked at me eagerly with hope and expectation. They actually seemed to think that this odd-looking person, by virtue of being clad in green coveralls and barn boots, would step in and magically put everything right.

My prayers were answered, but not in a way I would have expected. Dave turned to me and asked in his usual formal fashion, "Dr. Truelove, would you like me to restrain the patient?"

How perfect was this? Feeling that Dave might actually have more practical pig restraint knowledge from his education in the Midwest than I did, I calmly replied, "Yes, Dave, please do." Then I stepped back and watched to see what would transpire.

Dave had a brief discussion with the owners, and they all trudged up to the house leaving me to scratch my eyelid and stare at the blasted pig. I remembered a lecture where I was told that pigs often just need an added boost of oxytocin to help them expel the piglets. As long as the first piglet was not blocking the birth canal, administering a dose of this potent hormone was supposed to have spectacular results. More importantly, the results were non-surgical, which was particularly appealing to me. The only reason I remembered this factoid was that the professor who delivered it shared an aside with us. He had said that pigs are so sensitized to oxytocin that when given at the right time, it causes the piglets to be expelled with such force, "You need a catcher's mitt to grab them as they come out." You don't forget something like that.

If I could ascertain that nothing was blocking the birth canal, administer the hormone, and assist in the delivery, all should go well. Piece of cake, I tried to reassure myself. There were a few more moments of prayer to whoever controlled the porcine world, and then Dave and company reappeared with a door. It seemed the hinges had just been removed for the event, and I wondered what room of their house was now open to the breezes.

Good to his word, Dave maneuvered the sow into a restrained position presenting only her hindquarters to me. I asked the owner to bring warm, clean water. I cleaned her up, did a cursory examination, determined that there was no apparent blockage, and administered the initial dose of oxytocin. We waited for the moment of truth.

There is an art to conversation in these circumstances. As I already had found, exuding excess bravado was akin to asking for certain humiliation. On the other hand, conveying my true inadequate feelings to the owner would be unkind and unwise. As I remember, we made small talk about the hot weather, the price of pork, whatever came to mind as I anxiously watched my patient. It was difficult for me to look these people in the eye. They seemed consummately trusting in my abilities.

When I was close to despair and frantically wondering how this laboring sow may be transported to a more appropriate surgical environment, she sprang to action and gave a huge heave. I had one thought in my mind: "Catcher's mitt!"

I swung around, crouched behind her pudgy hindquarters, and was delighted to see a pink sack starting to emerge. Success! I grasped the piglet with gentle traction as I guided it out. I tore off the remaining fetal membranes and was delighted to see it gasp for air and start to turn a healthy pink color. My excitement was short-lived. As is the case for newborns, after they have a good lungful of air, they want to cry. The piglet let out a lusty squeal and the mother pig exploded. She appeared infuriated by the sound of her piglet's apparent distress. Dave was doing a heroic job of holding her in place as he leaned on his door wedged against her, blocking her from turning around. We had to prevent her from hearing any sound from the baby. I grabbed it, shouted to the owners to get it into the house *now*, and threw it like a peewee football into their waiting arms.

"*Run!*" I shouted. ("Run!" I thought later, seemed to be a common command when dealing with pigs.)

We quickly worked out a system to deliver the piglets, tear off the membranes, and get them safely into the house before their squealing incensed their mother. True to what I had been told, the oxytocin was magical in its effect. After the first stagnant piglet, they started firing out of the mother as if from the mouth of a canon. I grabbed, cleaned, tossed, and repeated the routine for piglet after piglet. During this chaotic time, my beeper, which was clipped to my coveralls, began beeping. There was no way I could stop and answer the call or even turn the thing off. I ignored it and went about my task. At some point as I was bending, scooping, twisting, and tossing, I heard the aggravating beep, beep, beep, turn to bloop, bloop, and then silence.

The damnable thing had come unclipped and fallen into the pig mire, slowly sinking and dying. I had decidedly mixed feelings about this.

Who knew that pig litters were so large? The process went on and on. We had no way of knowing when she was done. Adrenaline levels were off the charts. Finally, the sow seemed to relax, we had a prolonged quiet session, and then she started looking around expectantly. I gave her a scrutinizing look through my remaining good eye and called an end to the process. I quickly dug in the muck and retrieved the sodden beeper, called Dave off his post, and we exited the pen. The owners brought all fifteen of the piglets back and presented them to the delighted mother.

On the way back to the clinic, I expected Dave to have some excited comments about what had just happened. But as far as I could tell, this may have been the hundredth time Dave had watched and assisted pigging.

We cleaned up the vehicle and the equipment. I took the beeper and cleaned off the mud that I could reach. I opened it, cleaned the inside, and replaced the batteries. I tested it, but it was dead, a fallen soldier in combat. I had rented it from a service, so I made a trip to the office and dropped it off. They gave me a loaner while they serviced it.

Several days later, I received a call. They could not fix the beeper. They were very curious, though, as to what had happened to it. As I prepared to launch into a long explanation, I remembered that we had paid insurance on the unit and it would be replaced, regardless.

"Gee, I don't know," I said. "It started beeping and then sounded kind of funny and then stopped."

I wasn't sure if the insurance extended into the pig combat zone.

***

Potbellied pigs enjoyed a curious run of popularity for many years. Baby boomers, still remembering Arnold, were probably responsible for this phenomenon. Some brilliant individual launched a promotional campaign that promised the animals were cute, clean, and intelligent, easily trained, and were miniature versions of the usual farmyard pig.

All this was very true except for the last claim. I never saw a potbellied pig that didn't eventually grow to large proportions—perhaps not the size of pigs that are raised for meat, but bigger than anything you would want to keep in your home. Of course, by the time they've reached that size, they've become a beloved pet and the owners resign themselves to whatever accommodations they must make to ensure the pig's comfortable lifestyle.

My prospective patient was one of these fortunate piggys. He lived in the house with the family. His name was Dallas, and he was coming in for an evaluation of his recent seizure disorder. The owners were clear that they wanted to do anything to help their pet, including laboratory tests, X-rays, whatever I deemed necessary. This is usually good news for a veterinarian, but not necessarily when the patient is a pig, and you are working out of a small animal clinic. The logistics were daunting. I pondered how I would obtain a blood sample from this animal. The usual route is a large vein running on the surface of the ear. Needless to say, pigs strenuously object to having a needle inserted under the skin in their delicate ears. And when pigs object, they are not shy or quiet. Even if I were skilled and experienced in venipuncture on pigs, I couldn't imagine how I would do this in front of a sensitive owner without upsetting her.

It is also incredibly difficult to hold a pig. They are, after all, a giant tube of muscle covered in a heavy layer of fat. There are no convenient handholds. They can operate just as fast in reverse as in forward gear. In farm practice, a squeeze chute is generally used to hold them steady for procedures, and I certainly had nothing like that. What if I decided an X-ray were needed? How would I get the animal on the X-ray table? Even if we could, how would we ever hold it still for the procedure?

The obvious solution would have been to suggest the owners find a large-animal veterinarian, but my curiosity got the best of me and I knew that this was not a farm animal in the owners' eyes.

I had very little time to mull over my dilemma. The owners were bringing Dallas in that afternoon. I quickly dusted off some old textbooks to familiarize myself with normal parameters for pigs— temperature, pulse, respiration, (Dr. Fox would have been ashamed of me), and blood values. I checked on dosages for mild sedatives, antibiotics, anything I thought I might need. Having girded my loins, I waited.

Dallas arrived with full entourage. Both parents and two teenage children in tow, he strode into the waiting room full of curiosity and confidence. He was a pretty big pig, probably eighty to one hundred pounds of porker. He snuffed and grunted as he checked out the displays of food in the waiting room, and his owners filled out the information for his record. I invited them into the exam room, and as the wife passed me, she said, "Here, you're going to need this," and thrust a sandwich bag full of Cheerios into my hand. I eagerly awaited the explanation for the impromptu breakfast.

I spent lots of time taking the pig's history, avoiding the more difficult physical examination looming before me. Seizures can be problematic to address and much can be learned through history taking. The family was clearly devoted to their unusual pet. They were animated and anxious to answer all my questions. In interviewing them, I had entered a whole new world of pet ownership.

Dallas had been a perfect pig up until the last few weeks. He had never had any health problems or needed any veterinary care. Then, he had started having seizures during the night.

"Only during the night?" I asked.

"Yes, only at night."

"How do you know he's having a seizure if it's at night?" I foolishly queried.

"Because he sleeps on our bed," the husband answered.

They described the scene, and I struggled to keep my jaw from falling open in shock. It seemed that Dallas would jump up out of a sound sleep with his eyes wide and glassy. He would leap off the bed and run in circles, squealing all the time. It sometimes happened more than once on a given night.

I delved further into Dallas' lifestyle, trying to discern what was different at night that might be stimulating this bizarre behavior. They told me that he enjoyed watching television, but he was only allowed to watch *Mr. Rogers* and *Barney the Purple Dinosaur*. His favorite place was lying underneath a coffee table in the living room where he had a good view of the television. The family was planning to move soon, and in preparation, had sold some furniture they weren't going to bring along. Unfortunately, they had sold Dallas' table, and he had been visibly upset by its absence.

The plot was thickening.

I had asked all the history questions I could think of, and then turned to deal with Dallas, who had investigated every corner of the room and was apparently happy to sit and listen to us talk about him. I started toward him but the wife stopped me.

"Doctor? You forgot the Cheerios. You'll need them if you want to work on him. He'll behave himself and won't squeal if you feed him the Cheerios one by one as you examine him."

This was important knowledge and good planning on their part. I hoped I wouldn't run out of this valuable snack and wondered if their appeal was great enough to quiet him if I had to obtain a blood sample. Maybe I could introduce Fruit Loops for a novel distraction.

I examined Dallas, and as promised, he was entirely focused on the tiny tidbits I fed him. He delicately took each morsel from my fingers while I peered into his eyes and ears, and listened to his heart and lungs. I considered palpating his abdomen but it would clearly be an exercise in futility considering his girth, so I abandoned the effort. I even managed to take his temperature while a family member fed the Cheerios at a rapid rate at the opposite end.

Everything appeared normal to me, which is the case in most seizure disorders; laboratory tests are usually required to make any kind of diagnosis.

Just as I was bracing myself for mayhem, the husband calmly stated, almost as an aside, "We know what's wrong with him."

I wasn't going to pass this up, so I asked what he thought the problem was with Dallas.

"It all began after the kids had a sleepover. They stayed up all night watching Freddy Kruger movies and a twenty-four hour shark marathon. Dallas stayed up with them that night. He had never seen anything like that before, and he didn't have his table to hide under. The problem started right after that. I think he's having nightmares."

I looked up to see the other three family members nodding in agreement. As far as I was concerned, this case was closed. It did sound as if Dallas would be soundly asleep, wake up screaming (or squealing if you're a pig), and try to flee from whatever he had seen. What they had described, in retrospect, hadn't sounded like any form of seizure I was familiar with. The really inexplicable part to this scenario was why they had even bothered to come in for my opinion. Regardless, I was thrilled that the case of the terrorized pig was nearing its conclusions.

With a straight face, I got a prescription pad and wrote the following:

1. Try to track down Dallas' table and buy it back. If unable, go to a flea market and purchase something similar. Place it in front of the television.

2. Rent some *Barney* or *Mr. Rogers* videos and play them for Dallas during the evening up until bedtime.

3. Absolutely no violent or scary television-viewing while Dallas is in the house.

4. Call if seizure activity does not disappear within a week.

The happy family received my prescription with enthusiasm. I quickly poured the remaining Cheerios into Dallas' gaping mouth and they left to fulfill their assignments. The pig swaggered out of the clinic, corkscrew tail sort of wagging in a happy pig fashion. I only wish that I had watched them get into their vehicle. I will never know how a pig that size rides in a car. I never heard from them again, so I assume Dallas responded well to my prescription.

CHAPTER 7
Learning the Ins and Outs

Speeding down the interstate in a large animal "vet mobile," the reality of my situation sat like a cold stone in the pit of my stomach. It was one o'clock in the morning; I had never wanted to be in this position but had known that it would inevitably happen. Although I had worked hard in school and had done well, at this precise moment, I had a realistic grasp of what my true value was as a neophyte veterinarian in large animal practice. "Moose," my canine copilot was no help. He hung his head out the window, jowls flapping, sucking in the warm night air, ecstatic to be going for a ride. He thought I was brilliant because I could operate a can opener. Unfortunately, his opinion wasn't going to get me very far tonight.

My employer, a seasoned and extremely well respected dairy practitioner, would prime me for routine calls. He would take phone calls in the morning, confer with the farmers, and then make "armchair" diagnoses that were remarkably accurate. He would tell me what to check, what to use for treatment, even how to word my findings depending on the farmer whose herd I was treating.

Meanwhile, he was helping me build the farmers' confidence in me, the first female large animal veterinarian in the area. I happily swallowed any feminist pride and took this excellent preparation for what it was worth.

What truly terrified me, though, was the thought of emergency calls. The worst fear of all was treating a prolapsed uterus. In the dairy business, there are always many births. To maintain milk production, cows need to produce calves. Usually this process goes well, or needs only minor assistance from the farmer.

Sometimes it goes terribly wrong. Sometimes the cow expels the calf and the afterbirth, but fails to recognize the need to stop pushing. Eventually the entire uterus turns inside out and protrudes from the vulva. It is as horrible as one might fear. Imagine something like a stocking cap turned inside out and dotted with little mushroom caps hanging down below the cow's tail. Now, imagine that this mass is about the size of a large bushel basket and covered with blood, amniotic fluid, and organic debris found in the calving area. To make matters worse, the cow thinks she just needs to push a little harder to rid herself of this extremely uncomfortable protuberance. This is when the veterinarian is called.

It was my misfortune that I was never present to view treatment of a prolapsed uterus at vet school. Such was my fate that I had nothing but a classroom lecture and reading behind me when, shortly after my arrival in Vermont, an early evening phone call requested me to treat a prolapsed uterus. My employer, Jerry, graciously and wisely offered to take me with him so I could observe his technique.

He made it look *so* easy. He confined the cow in a dry area (we were out in a pasture) and the organ was thoroughly cleaned and disinfected. He adeptly administered a spinal anesthetic, and as if by magic, the straining stopped and the cow showed obvious relief. The veterinarian then unbuttoned his coveralls, rolled them down to his waist, and secured them with a piece of baling twine. This was his ritual, regardless of the season, so that he could clean up and be dry for his remaining calls. He then carefully inserted his right fist into the hollow of the everted organ, lifted it up to shoulder level, and asked the farmer to start pouring cups of hot water over it as the doctor kneaded the uterus around the opening of the vulva, pressing it slowly, slowly back inside. He explained that the hot water stimulated the muscle to contract, making it smaller and easier to replace.

Within no time, the cow looked like every other in the pasture. She received medication to prevent infection and was ready to go on her way. My employer, Jerry, washed up in a bucket of water, dried off, and replaced his coveralls. Except for the fact that this had all occurred under a constant barrage of mosquitoes, it had been downright civilized. I longed for the day when I could perform this feat so adroitly. To my dismay, I didn't have long to wait. It's one thing to watch someone with experience perform the miracle of returning the cow's anatomy to its former location, and quite another to do it yourself.

While on duty one night several weeks later, I received a call from a farmer reporting that one of his cows had a prolapsed uterus. Fortunately, I had been to his farm before, so I knew the location and that he seemed to be a very kind man. There was no chance of chickening out on this case and calling my employer for backup. It was after midnight, and I knew he had intended his earlier lesson to stick. I dressed, gathered my equipment, and left in the clinic truck. As I drove down the interstate, I desperately reviewed in my mind what I had previously observed. I was sure the owner would instantly see my amateurish attempts for what they were. My heart pounded faster, my mouth was dry, and I felt incapable of coherent speech. I looked at my dog sitting beside me in the truck and never wished so fervently that I could be a dog instead of a person.

I pulled into the dooryard of the farm and took a few breaths. I could not let myself contemplate how bad things might go. I steeled myself, stepped out, and began to collect my equipment from the back of the truck. Over my shoulder, I saw a dark figure lurch from the shadows. There was complete silence for a moment. I turned and to my relief it was the kind farmer. Somehow, he looked different tonight. As he began to speak, I realized why. He was inebriated!

"Waal, it's my best cow. Yup."

He stopped to steady himself with his hand on the fender of the truck.

"Soooons I saaww her, I gut her right in ta' stall."

At this point, he leaned into my face, cocked his head, and gave a little pathetic wink.

"I might's well tell ya. When I saw that booger was my best cow, I had a little drink!"

Enveloped in his breath, I felt *I* would probably fail a Breathalyzer test. He staggered off in the general direction of the barn, and I wasn't sure if I should carry my equipment or rush ahead to hold him up. He managed to negotiate the step into the barn, but just barely. He disappeared down the aisle between the herds of milking cows, and headed for a box stall at the end of the barn where he had confined my patient. Fascinated by his precarious journey, I almost missed one of the cows in her stanchion that had an obvious, filthy, bloody uterus hanging out of her and dangling in the gutter. I called out to him that the cow was actually in her stanchion, but he maintained he was *sure* she was in the stall.

Feeling I was in some surreal play, I stopped arguing with him and said, "Well, fine then, it looks like you have *two* cows with prolapsed uteri," and I began to unload my equipment. My first prolapsed uterus, and I wasn't even going to have a sober layperson in attendance who might give me some vital coaching. I wondered if this was punishment for transgressions in another life, but then I realized it was probably a blessing that he was inebriated. There was no way this poor man would recognize any mistake I might make.

I cleaned the cow, administered the spinal anesthetic and looked on, amazed, as the cow stopped straining and her tail became limp. You read the books, you understand the theory, but when you put it into practice and it actually works, it is awe-inspiring. Mumbling a mantra of "Oh, thank you, thank you, thank you," under my breath, I forged onward.

I was reaching the critical point. I wasn't sure I was strong enough to lift the organ, hold it in position, and keep it there long enough with one arm while I did the required manipulations with the other hand. Then I figured, if not me, then who? That was my job and it would have to be done.

I went into a focused mindset, positioned my right arm in the pouch, lifted it, found it was just as heavy as I had feared, and began to massage it. By now, my boozy attendant had abandoned his pointless watch over the normal cow chewing her cud in the stall and returned to a post near my patient. Remembering the hot water, I asked him if he might fetch me a pail full. He roused himself from his half-reclining position on the edge of the floor gutter and lurched off into the darkness. I wasn't sure I would ever see him again.

I was concentrating so intensely that I was unaware of how much time had elapsed, but I had reached the point that I was fairly certain I was making some headway with the wayward uterus. I could smell his breath before I sensed him at my shoulder. My water boy had indeed returned. Never taking my eyes off the uterus, as though eye contact was all that was maintaining its shaky perch, I asked him to start pouring the water over the uterus. Not having taken his mental state into account, I hadn't factored in his judgment, or lack thereof. He had drawn the water directly from the hot water tank and it was searing hot. He began to pour it over my arms and the uterus. I had to scream in his ear only three or four times before it registered through his alcohol haze that he should *stop*! I was sputtering and in pain from the scalding water, but absolutely refused to drop the uterus and lose my precious advantage.

He stopped and shrugged as if to say, "Women; just can't make up their minds," and resumed his station draped over the gutter's edge.

The uterus was back in. The cow looked good. But the farmer had a disturbing green tinge to his face and he kept belching. I, on the other hand, was floating on adrenaline and satisfaction. I replaced my equipment and headed for my truck. As I turned, he was there, and again, too close for comfort. He veered into my face. "Wanna' come inta' the house with me and clean up?"

I just wanted to get on my way, rehash in my mind all that had transpired, and get home to a shower. I thanked him very much but said I'd just be leaving. His eyes opened wider than I had seen them that evening, then a crafty little leer came over his face. "Oh! I don't mean nothin' by it. Ta' wife is in there. You don't have to worry about me!"

I almost burst out laughing at the thought. I wasn't sure the man could actually get up his porch stairs and through the door much less present any physical threat to me. He then offered to let me clean up in his milk house in the barn. Having had more experience with the hot water in there than I cared to think about, I just excused myself and left.

I sped home along the interstate, awash in my feeling of success. Intrigued by my new scent, Moose inched his way across the seat toward me. I didn't even realize how I looked until he started to lick my arm. I looked down and realized my arms and coveralls were saturated with blood and fluids. How would this look to a state trooper if I were stopped? I eased my foot back slightly off the accelerator.

***

Months later, I considered myself a fairly seasoned practitioner. Although I didn't relish the thought of replacing a prolapsed uterus, I did feel a certain degree of competence, having successfully replaced a number of them. They were not all as memorable as the first and certainly none had had such a bacchanal flavor to them. One Sunday afternoon I received an emergency call from a regular farm client. This was a very nice family farm established by a man who now ran it with his two young adult sons. The boys lived in houses on the property with their wives. Although born to a farm family, they were still young adults, and their father had not had a vacation from the farm and the milking in a very long time. He and his wife had finally decided to take a long awaited holiday and leave the farm to the boys for a weekend. It was a major move, entrusting the livelihood of three families to the assumed maturity of the boys. Of course, Murphy's Law dictated that this weekend would not go entirely without problems.

Friday night milking eased into Saturday, and then Sunday morning milking and the sons were feeling great about their abilities to run a dairy farm. But potential disaster struck Sunday afternoon when a valuable cow calved and then had prolapsed her uterus. They called me on emergency duty and I went right over.

I immediately sensed the young men were apprehensive about me. I hadn't done much work on the farm, and though they were fair and open-minded as were most of the Vermont farmers I had met, they wanted everything to go perfectly while their parents were away.

They asked if I replaced prolapses, "like Jerry."

I assured them that I did. They appeared only mildly reassured.

They had put the cow in a box stall with lots of clean bedding. I laid out my equipment, cleaned up the uterus, and administered the spinal anesthetic. The operation soon assumed a carnival atmosphere. The boys' bravado was taking over. They were perched on the fence around the stall with their respective wives, ready to fetch whatever I might need or toss in their critiques as necessary. A few neighbors had come over to watch as well. It was a still winter afternoon and between milkings, so nobody had much to do. The warm barn was quiet and the stall now ringed with expectant faces. The brothers were beginning to relax.

As I was about to begin the procedure, one of them said, "Now, you *do* replace prolapses just like Jerry, right?"

"Of course!" I assured him.

He grinned ear to ear, as this was exactly what he had hoped I would say. "Then I guess you'll be stripping to the waist about now, wontcha'!"

A big round of laughs followed, but I was not to be outdone by a young farm boy, so I responded, "Well, if I did that, I'd have to charge you a hefty entertainment fee in addition to the vet bill."

He looked me straight in the eye, hesitated just a moment, pulled off his cap, and started passing it around for a collection. There was a moment or two of embarrassed silence, and then one of the wives blurted out, "Whatever they'll pay you, we'll pay you more to leave it on!"

Somehow, this serious veterinary medical emergency had become a stage for stand-up comics! Sometimes things just happen to go really right for me. In school, my roommate and I were always bargain shopping for cheap clothes to wear under our coveralls. We had found sweatshirts with the Superman logo emblazoned across the chest. It was the '70s and we were in a vastly male dominated world. We couldn't resist, so for a laugh we each purchased one. I had cut off the sleeves and worn mine on farm calls off and on since then, as it was a highly expendable clothing item. This day, fate was definitely on my side. I remembered how I had dressed that morning and pondered a second. "Ladies, maybe they're right, I should do this prolapse 'just like Jerry.'"

I slowly unbuttoned the top of my coveralls. I watched their jaws slowly drop, and then I yanked back the top to reveal the Superman symbol on my chest. There were laughs all around, not the least of which came from the relieved wives.

CHAPTER 8
Patients That Go Walkabout

I was witnessing a canine version of Shawshank Redemption. A morning head count at the clinic turned up one short. The heavy wooden door that slid open to access our outdoor crematorium looked like a surfboard after a massive shark attack. The heavy wire fencing outdoors was twisted and torn back around a gaping hole large enough to accommodate a small farm animal. Veterinarians have lurking terrors in their professions and this appeared to be one of the "unexpected outcomes" that we dread. Of course, we fear losing a patient in the life or death sense, but we also sometimes lose them in the physical sense.

Animals can be amazingly clever but are even more impressive in their determination. Few animals enjoy the prospect of confinement to a limited area in a strange environment not of their choosing. Animals are creatures of the moment. They focus on themselves and their immediate situation. They are blissfully unconcerned with the plight of the world, taxes, the housing market, their weight, or getting their offspring into a good private school. Having few other concerns to occupy their time, they frequently dedicate every moment, every effort to escape. The crafty ones wait and make their move when they are unobserved, as any seasoned jailbird would. When they are successful, it ages a veterinarian.

This particular miscreant was a huge Neapolitan Mastiff admitted to the clinic for a minor skin problem. The owner had requested the dog stay with us overnight. Since we boarded dogs, we agreed.

He was a mammoth animal, weighing in at well over one hundred pounds. He was mottled gray and black with ears closely cropped against his skull. His head and jaws seemed to be the widest part of his body. Loose jowls hung down and periodically produced a long stream of saliva that glistened in the light until the dog shook its head, winding the strand around his muzzle. There was no doubt that this dog had presence. He did not merely occupy space, he loomed. Although he was sinister looking, having little expression in his small, shark-like eyes, he was passive to handle and seemed harmless. Due to his size, we felt he would be most comfortable spending the night in one of our enclosed runs rather than in a confining kennel. In the morning, we arrived to a scene of chaos and the realization of a bad choice.

Quickly evaluating the events of the evening, I realized that sometime after the last employee had left, the huge dog had managed to bend the heavy gauge fencing of his run and force its gate open. This had left him free in the larger room housing the runs. He had then found the opening in the cinder block wall covered by a heavy plywood sliding door; on the other side was our crematorium. With his massive jaws, he had actually chewed through the door until he was able to slide the door back on its track. Now close to freedom, he had made short work of the wire fencing around the crematorium. Our patient had gone walkabout. Panic set in. This bizarre looking beast was roaming the town. The Hound of the Baskervilles prowled the urban moors of Brattleboro, Vermont. We prayed he had not been injured. We offered counter prayers that he had not *inflicted* injuries, either.

As I was an employee of the clinic at the time, the brunt of the problem fell upon the owner. She quickly took action, jumped into her vehicle, and started to cruise the streets. I presumed she was driving one handed with her head hanging out the window, scanning every alley and parking lot. Although this sounded like a stressful assignment, it was no better back at the clinic. Concentration was impossible as the morning moved at a painful crawl. What were we to do if the owners showed up or called about their pet?

Thankfully, my employer eventually showed up at the back door of the clinic with a mortified expression and our vagrant patient on a leash. He looked unaffected, not a scratch, not a drop of blood, and surprisingly, absolutely no change in his impassive facial expression.

This dog was one cool character. He was Cool Hand Luke without Paul Newman's rakish good looks. Imagine Newman with the face of a gargoyle, a few strands of saliva wrapped around his face, smugly dragged back from his latest freedom flight.

While driving, my employer had begun to think that it was possible that the on duty town animal control officer had picked up the dog. At the time, we had no separate animal shelter in our town, strays boarded at local veterinary clinics. On a hunch, and resigned to swallowing her pride, she visited the other small animal clinic in our town and inquired about any dog that may have been admitted in the night. Her description didn't have to get beyond a few words when all faces lit up and they reassured her that they *definitely* had this dog in custody and would be very happy to hand him over. Of course, she had to pay the mandatory retrieval fee to the town, but this seemed a small price to pay in view of some other scenarios that could have played out. When he was discharged from our clinic, we respectfully informed the owner that their gargantuan pet would no longer be welcome as an overnight guest. His breakage fee, although unmentioned, had been excessive and surpassed even our stress levels.

***

Easing out of my warm vehicle into the frigid morning air, I was quickly aware of something being not quite right. The back door of the clinic was swinging open. Moving quickly down the hall, I found the radio on in the reception area, the telephone ringing, and no sign of a human being. Normally, my associate, two receptionists, a kennel attendant, a technician, and my husband would already be working. Hungry dogs barked in their kennels. Had I wakened to a scene from the *Twilight Zone*? Fighting an eerie feeling, I kept calling and looking. My mind filled with dramatic scenes of robbery or abduction. How could anyone force the entire staff to leave?

Eventually, the back door slammed and the technician ran down the hall. Even though it was well below freezing outdoors, she wore no coat, hat, or gloves. Her face and hands were blue, and she was gasping for breath. In bits and pieces, she shared the crisis of the morning.

A rather skittish German Shepherd had been in our care that evening. Built tall and rangy, he looked rather like a coyote. He had been extremely uneasy in the hospital, jumping at sudden noises and very reluctant to be handled by anyone on the staff. He was hyper-vigilant, constantly scanning every corner with flickering eye movements. It was apparent that this dog didn't get out much and certainly was not enjoying this visit to the bigger world.

While doing morning treatments, our kennel attendant mentioned that the dog seemed anxious about urinating in our enclosed runs. This happens occasionally with dogs that take their housetraining to the next level. They will hold their bodily functions until someone walks them outdoors. Not wanting to discomfort the dog any more, my associate took him outdoors to eliminate. We had a large area with a four-foot fence where we would take dogs and leash-walk them on these occasions. Holding the leash in one hand, my associate turned to fasten the latch on the gate, slipped on a patch of ice, and fell. The shepherd, immediately seizing the opportunity, pulled the leash from his hand and took off running around the pen. No attempt at reassuring him worked. The dog became increasingly agitated, eventually scaled the fence, and took off running toward the main road. At this moment, evocative of a hockey game, the benches emptied at the clinic. Every staff member flew out the doors attempting to retrieve the fleeing dog.

Fortunately, our patient made it safely across the busy road and dashed like a wild deer to cover behind the movie theater/store complex across the street. When staff members arrived, they found an entire hobo community living there. Who knew? At least we had spotters. They had seen the dog race by and said its direction was toward the frozen Connecticut River close by. Various staffers followed tracks for a very long time, but it became increasingly obvious that our dog had crossed the frozen river. When the staff returned to the clinic an idea presented itself. We looked at the dog's record card, and sure enough, he lived in a small town on the other side of the river. It was plausible that he had headed home.

Where is the section in the manual to cover this situation? What is the next reasonable step? I punted and made an executive decision. No matter how painful, I stuck to my belief that honesty is always the best policy. Gritting my teeth in anticipation of the reaction, I called the shepherd's owner. They were horrified. I assured them that our staff was in the field looking for their dog, but I suggested that they too should keep an eye out locally.

Thankfully, later in the day, I received a very chilly call informing me that the dog had arrived home. Tremendously relieved, I again did my utmost to apologize for this completely unexpected turn of events. Unfortunately, the owners informed me that their dog was limping. Later on, I examined the dog and found he had ruptured his anterior cruciate ligament, probably while scrambling over the fence. The runner ended up on my surgery table having the ligament repaired, gratis, of course. We never took him anywhere during that stay without two separate leashes and two guides at all times.

I was thankful that no lawyers came knocking on my door and that eventually the dog healed successfully. However, it reaffirmed my credo that it's best to tell the truth, no matter how painful for all parties concerned and get on with the outcome.

***

What you don't know certainly can hurt you. I do not like snakes, especially when they are out of their normal environment. I don't enjoy handling them and only do so if no other choice is presented.

One of my associates had a special interest in reptiles. He had a modest personal collection of pet specimens. His home was drafty and cold in the winter, so he chose to move his collection to an area in the clinic basement dubbed the Exotics Ward. It was quiet and cozy, as it was close to the furnace. He had asked permission to overwinter them there, and I was agreeable as long as I was not expected to minister to the snakes. I was relieved that my associate almost never asked for my help with his cold-blooded patients. In addition to a storage space in the basement, the area contained a small student apartment and a separate laundry area. Any time I had to go down there, I just avoided the Exotic Ward and everybody was happy. If I had only known.

One very warm Sunday afternoon in the early spring, my associate received an emergency call to appear at the clinic. He found two police cruisers parked at angles in the front parking lot. The officers were out of their vehicles and standing in a half circle, rigidly alert to something on the ground. He witnessed one of the officers poking and jabbing at the bushes in front of the clinic with a catchpole normally used to restrain aggressive dogs. The police officers' eyes bulged as they pointed into the patch of sun shining down on piled coils of smooth gleaming scales. They did not expect the response they got from my associate.

"Diva!" he cried out as he knelt down and gently lifted out the six-foot snake.

Unbeknownst to me, his large snake had escaped early in the

winter. He looked everywhere but was never able to find her. Knowing how phobic I was of snakes, he made the questionable decision to keep this news to himself. "Don't ask, don't tell" took on new significance. Somehow, Diva had spent the entire winter and early spring in the bowels of the building, and this sunny day she had found a way outside to take in some sunshine. As I was not in the habit of periodically asking, "So, Dr. Bob, are all of your reptiles accounted for today?" he never had to lie to me. Diva looked to be in top form, fat and glossy. We could only guess what she had been eating, but the clinic was certainly mouse free.

After his confession, I started to think of the "what if's" of the situation. What if I had gone rummaging through piles of laundry looking for a pet's blanket and unexpectedly found Diva? What if Diva had taken up residence on the heat pipes overhead, which she almost certainly would have, and had slipped down as I walked by? What if I reached into a storage box to retrieve an old X-ray and had instead grabbed Diva? My heart accelerates and my mouth turns to cotton even after all these years just contemplating these thoughts. Certainly, I would have suffered cardiac arrest on the spot. Eventually, my absence would have been noticed upstairs and someone would have found me in the basement, cold and gone, a contorted death shriek on my face. Diva would already have nonchalantly slithered off, and my demise would have just been chalked up as another untimely death.

***

Some escapes can be pure fun. A recently hired new weekend kennel attendant was young and enthusiastic. Her first Sunday alone at the clinic did not go well. I received an early morning call at home.

"Dr. Stronk! Dr. Stronk! There are two vicious dogs running loose in the clinic! I walked in the back door and they attacked me coming down the hall. I can't go back in there!" She had fled to the local convenience store and called me on a pay phone.

Concerned for her safety, I rushed to the clinic, unsure what I would face. The girl was so frightened that she had remained at the end of the driveway as though the feral beasts might burst out of the windows to get at her. Putting on my calmest face, I quietly unlocked the back door and eased into the clinic. I hoped I might be able to get a snare pole before I encountered one of the outlaws. I could not imagine how two dogs, both aggressive, could be running loose and wondered if they had been fighting with each other.

My terrified employee clung to my shadow, forcing herself to follow me into the jaws of death. As we rounded a corner into the large dog ward, two leaping, charging beasts, every tooth bared greeted us. Or so it seemed.

In truth, it was just Lowenbrau and Heineken, brother Keeshonds having a blast. The Keeshond breed has boundless energy, enthusiasm, and a huge "smile." When excited, and these boys were maxed out on happiness, they show every tooth in their head, and their lips curl up in a most disconcerting way. Mouths gaping open, tongues lolling out, they bore down on us. I stepped forward, grabbed their collars, one in each hand, told them they were bad boys, and needed to go back to their cage. They were crestfallen and meekly trotted along on either side of me. Their playtime was over.

My new employee looked at me as though I was the bravest person on earth. In her mind, I had instantly become a heroic figure. Lest she worship a false idol, I explained about the peculiarity of some breeds that smile, and I praised her for her caution, but assured her that these guys didn't have a mean bone in their bodies. They boarded with us often, or as we referred to it, they were "frequent fliers." They stayed in one large cage together. In bouncing around, they had popped the latch on the gate and had a wonderful evening exploring the clinic and cavorting through the halls. Imagine their delight when the back door opened and a new friend emerged. Of course, they charged the door, all smiles.

Some escapes remain mysteries. During morning treatments, we found a cat, spayed the previous day, now gone missing. Her kennel door was unlatched. We questioned the whole staff, but nobody had taken her out or had seen her that morning.

We stopped everything and began a thorough search of the clinic. As time passed, we began to run out of new places to look. We checked out all the obvious places and were now exploring places that seemed impossible. We peered down heating ducts with flashlights, opened large food tubs, anywhere a cat could physically fit. Everybody wanted to be the hero who found the cat, but it began to look dismal. We rechecked every space, emptied closets, and cabinets but found no feline.

I finally began to compose my dreaded call to the owner while I was doing some work in the lab. I had removed a form from a cabinet under the lab counter, and as I closed the door, my heart fluttered. Had I seen what I thought I saw? Having spent the last hour mentally visualizing a hiding cat, could my mind be playing tricks? Sucking in a deep breath, I slowly reopened the cabinet door and there, tucked between the top of the cabinet and the case for a flexible endoscope was, like the Cheshire cat, a pair of eyes glowing in the dark.

To this day, I do not know how or when the cat got in there. The cabinet doors fasten with a snap mechanism, not a magnet, so force from the outside is necessary to latch them, and conversely, the doors will not latch unless pulled from the inside. The cabinet was shut when we arrived in the morning and discovered that the cat was missing. We had emptied the cabinet early in our search and replaced its contents. The cabinet had no inner vent areas through which the cat could enter, but for all I cared, the cat could have telekinetically transported from her kennel to the cabinet. I was just delighted that I did not have to make that phone call. Sometimes solutions are far superior to answers.

***

Brattleboro has received a small amount of national renown for staging our annual Strolling of the Heifers down Main Street. It is a little known fact that I was personally responsible for the genesis of this concept. Unfortunately, I am the only person aware of this, but I feel compelled to reveal its true origin, at least as it exists in my mind.

In the early days of the clinic, we had a large animal facility situated on the property. Although the clinic was on a busy main street leading into Brattleboro along with strip malls and gas stations, we had good accommodations for farm animals. We had cows come in for surgical procedures, and it sometimes housed various horses, sheep, or pigs.

Livestock trucks via a loading ramp easily accessed the clinic, and there were paddocks in back so our patients could exercise and graze. Things usually went very smoothly, but the one time in my memory that they did not, it was surreal.

We routinely performed surgery on cows who had twisted one of their four stomachs. After surgery on one such patient to correct the situation, a livestock transporter had been engaged to take her home later in the day. She still needed to be milked, so I went out to put her in the barn where she would be milked in a stanchion. In the process of attempting to convince her that she needed to go into the barn, she became extremely belligerent. Probably remembering her last trip in there when she had her surgery, she became quite resistant to the idea. Suddenly she spun around, amazingly agile for a bovine of her size, and so recently postoperative, she rammed through the gate blocking the loading ramp used by the trucks. Ears and tail held high, she trotted up the ramp, hopped off the drop at the end like a seasoned cross-country horse, and loped up the driveway to the road.

Madness ensued. It's one thing to round up a cow out on the prairie or in a field with your trusty cowpony or even pursue her with an all-terrain vehicle. But how does one go about corralling an animal trotting down the main street into the city among cars with her over-full udder bobbing from side to side between her hind legs?

If nothing else, veterinarians are intrepid and necessarily fast thinking. Quickly, we mustered everything at hand that might be of use. There was one pick-up truck in the lead, people crammed into the bed of the truck (not many of whom had any clue about cow handling), armed with halters and buckets of grain, and a follow-up chase vehicle. Kennel staff, receptionist, those physically able to stay on their feet and potentially face down a charging half ton of ticked-off Holstein, were employed.

With all our efforts of speeding ahead, dropping people with halters and grain at promising intersections, and waving down traffic, our fast traveling cow was eventually apprehended. The person who suffered the most was the one who had to hike back through town leading the cow that now appeared to possess only one gear, an agonizingly slow motion stroll. Thriving on her new fame, she sashayed along the pavement, udder swaying seductively, hips rolling, huge, long lashed dark eyes gazing out over the admiring crowd, and basking in her milieu. She was a four-legged Helen of Troy returning from victory in her small battle for freedom. Meanwhile, at the other end of her rope, I was truly "cowed."

CHAPTER 9
Rx: A Daily Dose of Embarrassment

Speechless, I stand in horror watching the result of my good work turn to ruin. A trickle of oily water runs down the driveway as I desperately try to form some words. The sirens of pride have called me insistently and once again, I am swept up in their spell. Once more, I will have to pay the price. How can I be such an idiot?

Those in the medical professions are looked upon for guidance. It is easy to become enmeshed in the image of the white lab coat and to believe we have some mystical power. In my case, of the seven deadly sins, hubris is my downfall. Life is full of checks and balances, and in veterinary medicine, there is no shortage of four-legged beasts to put us back in touch with reality.

In my first year in practice, I was anxious to build up the equine clientele of the clinic that employed me. Historically known as a bovine practice, the doctors were willing to do a little horse work if necessary. I, on the other hand, loved horses and felt that I could be an asset to our hospital. I would jump to take any call requesting care for a horse and made every effort to impress the owners while ministering to their equines. During this time, I was on emergency duty on a Sunday afternoon and received an urgent call from an upset horse owner who had never used our services.

The owners had been at a horse show most of the day and had returned home to find one of their young horses thrashing in pain from colic. Their regular veterinarian was out of town. They knew this could be a life-threatening situation and called us for help. I agreed to come and quickly set out.

I arrived at a prosperous-looking establishment and immediately saw my patient being walked around the yard. He was reluctant to move and frequently turned his head to look at his flank. He would try to drop down and roll on the ground, but the owner, knowing how detrimental this could be, kept the horse on his feet. I jumped from my truck, collected my gear, and hurried to introduce myself and get to work.

I could see that the owner was concerned that I was new to her and obviously quite young. She tried to slip in questions about my background and my experience between answering health questions about her animal. I tried to be as reassuring as possible and hoped my performance on this case would speak for my capabilities.

I examined the colt and gave the owner my findings. I administered some pain medication and an antispasmodic to help relieve the horse's extreme distress. He relaxed slightly.

When a horse is suffering from colic, it is helpful if he can empty out the content of his gut, eliminating anything that may be responsible for the symptoms. To that end, we administer warm mineral oil—not a little mineral oil, a *lot* of mineral oil. The standard dose was one gallon. As may be expected, horses do not belly up to the bar and suck down a gallon of mineral oil of their own volition. This is the art of veterinary medicine at its best. The mineral oil is administered through a stomach tube passed into the horse's nostril, down its esophagus, and into its stomach. Then, held in place, the oil is pumped in. The potential hazards are many, and I'm only talking about the patient, not hazards to the doctor. Horses do not enjoy a long tube that is only slightly thinner than a garden hose passed through their nostrils. During the passage process, the horse, understandably, has a tendency to fling his head, snort, and do anything else to prevent this abomination from happening. If these gyrations rattle the tube excessively while it is against the delicate nasal membranes, or if the operator is too heavy-handed in passing the tube, a nosebleed of epic proportions results. Horse owners do not like this.

Once the tube is moving along the nasal passage, the biggest hurdle of all lies ahead. As the tip reaches the larynx, the horse must actively swallow the tube so that it progresses into the esophagus. If the horse does not swallow the tube, it can pass down the trachea. If this is not corrected, one gallon of mineral oil will be pumped into the horse's lungs, and he will die suddenly and horribly. Horse owners really, really do not like this.

The risks are not over yet. Hopefully we had measured the distance from the nostril to the region of the stomach ahead of time and marked that spot on the tube. If the tube isn't in the stomach, oil could flush back up the esophagus and be inhaled. If it is passed too far, there is a chance the tube will double back on itself, and again, flush oil into the esophagus.

With the tube in place, the doctor steadies it where it disappears up the nostril, grasps the open end, and blows into it briefly. As soon as the tube comes out of our mouth, we place the end under our nose and inhale deeply. This is not voodoo medicine. We are actually sniffing to detect telltale gastric contents. If the air that blasts back smells like grass or grain or even fermenting apples, we know the tube is safely in the stomach. We have also received valuable information about what the horse may have eaten that led to this medical interlude.

The last step involves audience participation. Since the vet is busy immobilizing the tube in the nostril, he or she is unable to operate the stomach pump, a two-handed process. This pump is, essentially, a stainless steel bilge pump. The open end of the tube is attached to the top of the pump. The end of the pump is put at the bottom of a stainless steel bucket containing the gallon of mineral oil. The lovely assistant then starts pumping the handle at the top of the pump. The mineral oil is sucked from the bucket and delivered directly to the patient's stomach with each pump of the handle. It doesn't take long to empty the contents of the bucket. The tube is then gently removed and the process is complete.

Experienced equine practitioners can do this entire procedure in their sleep. (And some probably do on overworked occasions!) However, there is a great deal of finesse and planning involved. It is also helpful to be a "horse person" with a calm demeanor that inspires confidence and tranquility in the patient. Although relatively inexperienced, I tried to be all this for the worried owner on a bright summer afternoon.

I sensed trepidation in the air as I prepared my equipment. I slung the tube around my neck and grasped in my teeth the flared end that would attach to the pump. This was how I had seen many accomplished equine practitioners do it and felt this would inspire confidence on the owner's part.

The tube passed through the nostril with no problem. My patient was anxious but cooperative despite his youth. I paused at the crucial swallowing point, and to my delight, the colt gulped at just the right time. I watched the tip of the tube move smoothly down the groove on the side of his neck and descend toward his stomach. I had thought to mark the tube before starting and stopped at my mark. I took the tube from my teeth, blew into it, and smelled the reassuring green grass smell. I passed the end to the owner. She was an experienced equestrian and she knew the drill. Quickly, she attached the tube and began to pump. The oil in the bucket slurped and shuddered with each stroke of the pump and soon disappeared. I gently slid the tube from the horse's nostril and noted with no small degree of pride that there was not a drop of blood, and my patient still appeared calm and unperturbed.

Basking in my performance, I stayed for a while to watch my patient and reassure all of us that he was feeling better. I asked to have my bucket filled with hot water so that I could clean up my equipment. The owner, still nattily attired in a button-down shirt and a skirt she must have worn for the horse show (where I assumed she functioned as a riding instructor or possibly even a judge), walked off to fetch a bucket. I allowed myself to gloat a bit and wondered if she might be tempted to call me the next time she needed a veterinarian. Surely, she would mention to other horsey friends what a competent job I had done with her young show prospect in his time of need.

The woman returned with a bucket of hot water, and I dropped the oily pump into it. I started to talk to her about follow-up care for the colt, such as diet and exercise, as well as any indications that she might need to call me back for further care. As I carefully organized my instructions for her, I mechanically began cleaning. With absolutely no forethought, I filled the pump with the hot water and oil mixture. Unfortunately, I had forgotten that the pump moved fluid at great velocity, both on the downward pump *and* the upward pump. As I pulled the pump handle up, the water and oil blasted out the top of the pump as if from a fire hose. It was supremely unfortunate because my cherished client was standing directly in front of it. The blast hit her squarely in the crotch region of her stylish skirt.

What could I say? A mere apology wouldn't even scratch the surface. I felt like a complete nincompoop. She stood there for a very long time with her mouth open and the oily mess dripping down all around her. She finally spun around and headed back to her house. I flung my remaining gear into the truck, my cheeks on fire. She eventually returned in a change of clothes. I couldn't look her in the eye. Not a word was spoken about the incident, and I drove off praying fervently that the colt would recover and not force this poor woman to have to dial my number again. Ever.

***

Oddly, negative experiences tend to burn more deeply in my memory than some of the more positive experiences do. Attempting to benefit from these painful episodes has made me a kinder and gentler person with my fellow practitioner, or at least that is my hope. Nobody is immune because none of us is perfect.

Shortly after we purchased our clinic, we employed a young female veterinarian. She was certainly a competent practitioner for her few years in practice. In particular, she felt she was knowledgeable about canine reproduction. As I had practiced quite a bit in this specialty, clients who bred their dogs usually requested my services. I knew she was a bit envious of my position and looked forward to being the veterinarian to call regarding canine procreative interludes.

My associate's time came with a call from a new client with a bloodhound that he intended to use as a stud dog. Prior to offering the dog's services, he needed to have a sample of his semen evaluated to ensure that the dog was potent. Our young practitioner had made an appointment for the owner to bring in his prized hound to have a sample collected and evaluated. I saw the appointment on the calendar and casually asked my associate if the client was also going to bring along a female dog in estrus to entice a performance from our new patient.

This was always a logistical problem. Male dogs need some prompting to put them in the mood. There are no doggie "girlie magazines" to stimulate their impulses. Especially with young dogs and in an unfamiliar environment, the olfactory and visual cues are critical to getting a good sample. There never seems to be a female dog at the special hormonal peak when we need one. This makes scheduling such appointments difficult at best.

As soon as I asked about the arrangements, I could see a sudden look of concern cross my associate's face. But she tossed her head, quickly put on a confident demeanor, and announced it wouldn't be necessary. She would be capable of doing the job without a bitch. I decided to chalk up the upcoming encounter to tough love on my part and I let her proceed.

On the appointed day, we were shorthanded for help. The massive bloodhound arrived with the owner in tow. There were no assistants available at the time to help, so my associate asked if I minded coming in the examination room to hold the dog while she performed her collection. I said I'd be happy to help. Of course, I was thrilled with the prospect of witnessing the spectacle. If she succeeded where most failed, I could be first to shake her hand. If she failed, as I was fairly certain that she would, I could just smile like the Cheshire cat and say nothing. Either prospect looked pretty satisfying to me.

The collection apparatus was laid out and all was ready. This dog easily weighed in at one hundred and twenty pounds so there was no considering putting him on the exam table. My associate explained the process professionally to the owner, assumed her position next to his flank, faced backward, and started her manual enticement to perform. As is usual in these cases, the room became very quiet. No conversation seems appropriate at the time, and unnecessary chatter can distract the dog. Even on the canine level, there must be some consideration of sensitivity. Time passed. Nobody moved or spoke. Then I saw my associate reach for the artificial vagina. "We're almost ready," she whispered.

I had to admit that I was very impressed when suddenly a deep guttural noise rumbled and seemed to shake the very walls of the room.

I quickly looked to our patient's head. His chin was resting on the crossbar under the exam table. His velvety jowls were draped over the bar and hung down in an oddly graceful way. His big soulful eyes were closed and he was *snoring!*

I don't know if I was more amused by the fact that the dog had been whipped into a state of somnolence rather than sexual excitation, or that my colleague was so sure that Old Faithful was about to blow just as the dog entered rapid eye movement (REM) sleep.

CHAPTER 10
The Troll

Dr. Arnie was chuckling and shaking his head before I could even finish telling him about my recent stable visit. Worse, everyone else in the treatment room was doing the same. What was wrong with them? This had been a very distressing event for me and they acted as though it was a joke of some kind. Feeling very annoyed, I asked what they thought was so funny.

"Robin, that's what I love about your stories. You exaggerate so much they're even funnier."

Exaggerate? The line had been drawn in the sand. The gauntlet was on the ground before me. I would show him this was no exaggeration.

Working in a mixed animal practice with a delightful employer had been wonderful. Dr. Arnie was a great mentor, supportive and helpful, and he appreciated my sense of humor. He was the perfect yin for my yang as a budding practitioner. He was tall and quiet, radiating an aura of serious concentration. I was younger, more animated, and anxious to show him that I could be an asset to his practice.

Clients would gravitate toward one or the other of us. It was an enjoyable work environment. His large animal practice was mainly equine, and we provided service to some very nice stables. I strove to keep the clients happy with our practice and tried to expand to include new clients. Being a veterinary rainmaker was my goal. Sometimes I might have tried too hard.

We had a pre-veterinary student with us who was observing and helping when possible. This was a common practice, and often we would be as inspired by the neophyte's enthusiasm as he or she was stimulated by the work. The students were all individuals and some contributed more than others did.

This student was a young woman who never said much. She was ever attentive and scurried about as we worked. It was an effort to try to engage her in conversation, so we often just let her watch and ceased wondering what she might be thinking. Nobody resented her presence; she was just part of the background at times. She was very short and rather square. We did not intend any ill will, but we had taken to calling her The Troll.

During this time, word had gotten out that a previously abandoned stable in the next town had been purchased and was under renovation. It soon became clear that it was going to be a hub of equine activities. The new owners provided boarding facilities, lessons for many levels of expertise, and sold and bought horses.

Large stables usually find a veterinarian they work well with and then give that individual all their business. I thought it would be a fine feather in my cap if I were to bond with the owners of this stable.

I was delighted one day to receive a call from a client who was considering purchasing a horse stabled at the new establishment that had been the object of my fascination. I sensed an excellent opportunity. "Vetting" a horse is a very important process. Prospective horse buyers engage a veterinarian to determine if the animal is suitable and sound for their intended purpose. We are usually informed of the stated sale price, as this helps us decide how intense our scrutiny must be. An older pony priced at five hundred dollars that is expected to carry children around the backyard gets a good exam. A ten thousand dollar, three-day event prospect, gets a much more extensive evaluation, usually including X-rays, blood tests, ultrasound exams, and more.

The horse I was to examine was to be the first horse for the family's daughter. She wanted to take lessons on it, trail ride, and possibly go to some 4-H events. This should have been a fairly basic exam. But in my overzealous state, I saw opportunity written all over this farm call. That barn would be my stage, and I intended to work the crowd.

On the appointed day, I left plenty of time to ensure that my entrance would be punctual. As always, The Troll road shotgun. After I told her the purpose of the call, she found no further cause for conversation. I was lost in my plans of glory and left her to her musings.

It was Saturday morning and the stable was a beehive of activity. Classes were in full swing, parents, children, friends were everywhere. The blacksmith was even on hand. Oh, happy day, I thought; by the end of this exam, everybody must agree that this young veterinarian is just what the stable needs. Surely, hints will be dropped to the stable manager, and I can proudly hand this new account over to the practice.

After I chatted with the parents, the equine candidate was brought out for my evaluation. I scrutinized, poked, prodded, and pondered every square centimeter of the beast. I kept up a constant line of prattle so everyone around would understand what a solid grasp I had of this procedure and would feel they had received some valuable knowledge.

I used the ophthalmoscope and peered into the deep layers of his eyes. I carefully applied the hoof testers to all four feet to look for hidden areas of sensitivity. I examined his teeth as if they were my last vision on earth, and I wanted to memorize every tiny detail. No joint went unpalpated, flexed, extended, and critiqued. I told the growing crowd how we could be sure that the horse did not suffer from various afflictions and the significance of these findings. I drew blood samples and smiled inwardly as I quickly placed the needle in the jugular vein with no response from my patient. The crowd was mine and I was thrilled. They hung on my every word.

Although I had spent plenty of time listening to the horse's heart and lungs, I explained to my audience that it was important to exercise the horse to increase the heart rate and get the horse breathing deeply so I could listen again. Like Moses parting the Red Sea, I asked for room so the horse could jog up and down for a while. The excitement increased as people became genuinely invested in knowing if it was "deal or no deal."

The horse came back nicely invigorated, and I put on my stethoscope and went to work. I was enjoying the absolute silence and the expectant faces all awaiting my verdict. I had informed them that this was the last part of the examination.

I removed the stethoscope from my ears, folded it carefully, and placed it in the back pocket of my coveralls. After a theatrical pause, I began to relay my findings: all were positive. As I spoke, I had an odd sensation that I had trouble localizing. I continued to speak but was distracted somehow. I suddenly realized that I couldn't hear anything in my right ear. I was puzzled for a moment, and while speaking, slid my hand up to my right ear as if to chase a fly. I allowed my finger to rest inside my ear for a second and my heart sank. If I had this scene to repeat, I would have continued with my discourse, but we never enjoy the gift of hindsight. I nonchalantly reached back into my coverall pocket and casually removed my stethoscope. Sure enough, the right earpiece was gone!

Stethoscopes have round, white plastic earpieces that screw onto the instrument. They come in different sizes and user's can change them to their satisfaction. The operative word in this description is round. Suffering from a severe case of overconfidence, I figured I could extract the earpiece as I spoke and nobody in the crowd would be the wiser.

Again, I casually motioned as though repelling a fly, made a quick foray into my ear, and dug at the foreign body expecting it to pop out immediately. All it did was roll around, nestled tightly in the canal. Unfortunately, I have always been tenacious and this was no time to give in to a mere piece of plastic. As I resumed my efforts, I fear my discourse may have suffered. My eyes may even have been rolling just a tiny bit following the lack of progress of the earpiece. I saw someone nudge someone else in the crowd and nod toward me. There were a few audible snickers.

Now I *couldn't* stop. My pride was on the line. A few people actually laughed. It was clear what my predicament was. I was mortified. I could feel the heat wave coming out of the collar of my coveralls and engulfing my face. My cheeks were twin lanterns. I quickly concluded my overlong evaluation of the horse, rapidly threw all my equipment helter-skelter into the bag, and made a hasty retreat out of the stable. I drove off as quickly as I could, unable to look back.

As I drove down the road, I had time to contemplate the outcome of pride and overconfidence. What had turned me into such an idiot? I was sure they would talk about me plenty at that stable, but it would all be about what a clown I had been. I was thinking about how I would tell Dr. Arnie about this travesty when I glanced over at the passenger's seat and realized I had forgotten The Troll and left her behind!

This certainly added insult to injury. I quickly turned and drove back to the stable. I couldn't face them again. I should have known better. As I pulled into the stable yard, there was The Troll, like a faithful pet dog, sitting patiently on the porch step waiting for me. She got into the truck without a word, and we drove back to the clinic in our customary silence. For once, the silence was sweet.

The earpiece, still lodged in my ear, had to come out somehow. There was no way I was going to break the code of silence and ask The

Troll to assist me. Back at the clinic, I grabbed a forceps from a surgical tray and hurried off to the bathroom for a moment of abject solitude.

When I emerged, the culprit was in the palm of my hand. Staring down at the hateful thing, I could almost imagine a little smiling face on it, gloating with triumph.

Later on when I did tell Dr. Arnie the story, he had a hearty laugh. Exaggerate? I was stunned by this observation. Without hesitation, I fetched a stethoscope, unscrewed the earpiece, and handed it to him. I asked him to place it in his ear and then remove it. He smiled indulgently and put it in his ear. Then he reached up with the same smug look I must have had and made his initial attempt at extraction. Nothing. He wiggled his finger, he changed positions, and he held his head to the side. Nothing. I watched his eyes roll, his uncontrollable grimace as he felt he almost had it but it slipped. Part of me felt vindicated by his gyrations, but part of me was in mortal dismay that that was exactly how I had looked to the assembled multitudes that black Saturday morning.

When I finally got a forceps and removed the earpiece, I was certain I wouldn't have to hear anything about my exaggerated stories again.

CHAPTER 11
Black Jack's Broken Rib

"Why do you think the horse's rib is broken?" I asked the caller.

"Because it's sticking out," he replied.

"Is it located in the saddle area?"

"No, it's back by his rump."

"There are no ribs back there," I informed him.

"But it's sticking out," he insisted.

Very often things are not what they seem and this can be especially true in veterinary practice. We are more surprised, maybe even disappointed, when things *are* what they seem. When the animal in question is miles away from the doctor and communications are handled over the telephone, the outcome can be confusing and sometimes quite hysterical. The caller may be confused by what they are seeing and misinterpret. Or the caller may be upset or embarrassed by what they see. In this case, the owner was just painfully literal in his response to my inquiries.

A horse is a very tough animal and the incidence of broken ribs is rare. It would take an incredible amount of blunt trauma to fracture a rib that lies nicely protected under a dense mass of muscle and fat. I had never heard of a horse that had broken a rib without a history of massive trauma. I did not have a practiced line of interrogation to cover this topic.

Concerned about the overall condition of the horse, I asked, "Is the horse eating?"

"Not right now."

Trying to create a mental image of what might be wrong, I asked, "How big is the opening in the skin?"

"The skin isn't open."

"Then you just see a bump?"

"Yeah."

Now, I felt, we may be getting somewhere.

"How big?" I asked.

"Pretty big."

This was a man of few words. I began to long for the chatter of my more garrulous clients who would have told me far more than what I needed to know at this point. I was becoming frustrated.

"How big is pretty big? An egg? An orange?"

"Well, he's a pretty big horse," was his succinct reply.

I realized that we could play this game all day, but I would undoubtedly need to go examine the unfortunate beast. I would have to squeeze him into my afternoon of farm calls.

"Where is the horse kept?" I asked, trying to arrange my itinerary.

"In a stall."

I kicked myself for setting myself up. I should have anticipated that response by now. This caller did not intend any disrespect or to be a wise guy. He was genuinely doing the best job he could to answer my questions. I could probably have asked him the capital of North Dakota and he would have had an answer and have seen no problem with my line of questioning.

When we finally reached a meeting of the minds where he gave me directions to his farm, I was pretty sure I recognized where it was, but needed to confirm the exact location.

"Is it a big stable?" I asked.

"Yeah, it used to be a chicken coop ... it's pretty big."

I began getting a little apprehensive about this medical mystery and thought of one more brainteaser.

"What shape is the lump?"

"Well, kind of rib-shaped, you know?"

Well, that explained everything.

I couldn't wait to meet this engaging conversationalist in person. I gave him an approximate time that I would arrive at his equine Taj Mahal, and then I packed up the truck and hit the road.

By the time I arrived, it was dark. The really troublesome cases always manage to materialize under the cover of darkness. And of course, it was cold. It was winter; damp, raw weather that chilled your bones, even broken rib bones.

My new phone friend met me and led me down into the bottom level of what indeed had once been a commercial chicken operation. The ceiling was extremely low. I'm average height, but I found myself walking with my knees slightly bent to avoid the possibility of knocking myself out on support beams. I wondered what his phone call to 9-1-1 might be to report an unconscious veterinarian. I was sure he wouldn't say I had a broken rib.

Several farm animals were loose and milling around in the

semidarkness. A few dim lightbulbs coated with flyspecks glowed weakly in spots that did me no good.

The horse's owner led the way with a flashlight and finally brought me to my patient. Although not restrained in any way, the horse was, in veterinary terms, "reluctant to move." He may as well have been nailed to the floor. He stood rigid, not twitching a muscle. Squinting in the dim light, what to my wondering eyes should appear but a firm lump jutting up in the horse's flank, just in front of his hip.

At this point, I'd like to say I smiled calmly and said, "Aha! Another one of these cases!" But in reality, I thought something more like, "What the heck?"

I hesitated to open my mouth because some pretty unintelligent possibilities were running through my mind. No wonder the poor guy figured it was a rib and went from there. My thoughts weren't much better, and I had been trained.

I lightly touched the bulge. It was clear the horse did not appreciate this contact. His ears were pinned back, his teeth exposed, and his tail slashing, he still refused to move. For this, I was grateful. The lump was hard. Very hard, like a rock (or a rib?).

I cleared my mind and ran down a list of possibilities. It was woefully short. Suddenly I had an epiphany. The horse's name was Black Jack, and the owner had referred to the horse as "he," but with all the other wealth of information I had received, there was always a possibility that this was incorrect. What I had felt could have been a foal's hoof. What if it was really a mare that had been accidentally bred, ruptured her uterus, and the foal's leg was sticking up?

Although there is some line of logic here, I am embarrassed to have committed that thought to paper, but it is true that I briefly entertained it. However, it did lead to the clue that solved the mystery. With this dreadful thought in mind, images of heroic life-saving efforts, unthinkable surgery, or even euthanasia flashed before my eyes. With trepidation, I slowly stooped to look at the horse's belly, ready to announce that Black Jack was actually Black Jill when I noted a small pool of dark fluid in the straw under the horse. And, yes, there was a full complement of male gear attached to the underside as well, blowing my theory out of the water.

Watching closely, I saw an occasional drip issue from high up in the horse's groin and land in the pool. I grabbed the flashlight, twisted around under the horse, and saw a small raw wound just inside the fold of the flank in the belly.

Now things were beginning to gel. This horse must have impaled himself on something that had broken off inside him. It was incredible that he was standing there at all. From my angle, it appeared almost certain that the abdomen had been penetrated. This was not good, but at least it was explainable.

However, there was no way I could do anything in this environment. For starters, it was unimaginable that the horse put up with a situation where he couldn't even raise his head fully because of the low ceiling. Furthermore, any care would have to be administered in a much more hygienic and well-lit area. Having stray goats and chickens wandering through a surgical field was definitely unacceptable. The owner would need to take the horse to our clinic where I could explore the wound and the foreign body and be prepared to do whatever surgery might be indicated.

Fearing the logistics of getting the wounded horse out of the coop and shipped several towns away to our clinic would be impossible, I asked the owner if he could get him there by morning. He responded in his inimitable style.

"Yeah."

This guy was beginning to grow on me. I administered a tetanus vaccination, antibiotics, and pain medication and left to spend a sleepless night wondering what Pandora's box would reveal if I got as far as opening it.

In the morning, good to his word, the owner delivered Black Jack to the clinic in a sketchy looking livestock truck. In the light of day, the horse looked pretty good. I gave him a thorough physical exam and took his history. Efforts at history taking didn't last long. I had learned a lot from my new client as far as reasonable expectations. The one question he was able to answer was his horse's age; he thought it was ten years old. This was encouraging, as ten is the prime of life for most horses, giving him a robust chance at survival. Just for fun, I lifted Black Jack's lip to give myself a second opinion on his age. My bubble burst as it became clear from the wear on his teeth that Black Jack would have been old enough to vote in the last election. I hoped that he came from a particularly long-lived lineage of equines.

I administered a heavy dose of tranquilizer/pain medication and led Black Jack into a restraint chute. We didn't do large animal surgery often in the clinic and our small animal technician, Pat, was very excited to help. On rare occasions, when our large animal assistant wasn't available, Pat would come out on farm calls with us. She had seen a few cows treated and loved horses.

After clipping the hair and cleaning the area, I started the serious work. I was concentrating on Black Jack, administering a local anesthetic over the offending lump and explaining aloud to Pat what I was doing as I proceeded. She was very anxious to help and was ready for anything.

Poised on top of an upturned bucket, I surveyed my surgical field. After putting on my surgery gloves, I draped the area with sterile towels and grasped my scalpel. Taking a deep breath, I asked Pat to steady the horse's head. I cut through the skin of the flank and quickly exposed the culprit: the butt end of a big wooden stake. On the uppermost end of the stake was a little fuzzy crown of tan belly fur that had been driven up under the skin with the stick. The diameter of the stick was wider than a shovel handle. The owner had been the master of understatement when he called it "pretty big." My respect for the fellow grew and grew.

I had sterilized a pair of plier-type instruments ahead of time and used them to grasp the end of the stick. I gently pulled. And pulled. And pulled. Suddenly visions of the Banana Man on the old *Captain Kangaroo Show* came to mind. He would reach into the bottomless pockets of his baggy coat and produce endless chains of bananas. And so it was with this stick. I kept pulling and more and more of the stick inched its way reluctantly out of the incision. The stick ended up being fifteen inches long. The sharp point was at the bottom end, defying any explanation of why it was driven in this way. Nevertheless, it was out and that was what mattered now.

The abdomen did not appear penetrated. The stick seemed to have reflected along the abdomen under a layer of skin, fat, and muscle. I flushed disinfecting solution down through the opening and heard it run down onto the ground at the horse's foot. Mission accomplished. Before I started to suture the wound, I refocused on my willing assistant.

As I looked to Black Jack's head, I couldn't believe what I saw. Pat had put her fingers in each of his nostrils, pincer fashion, grasped his head and pulled it around toward her where she had been holding it firmly for the entire procedure. This is a fairly common restraint technique for cows; they allow it and respond in a docile manner. Horses are completely different and normally do not tolerate any manipulation that involves touching inside their nostrils. Having only been on cattle visits, Pat thought this was standard procedure for any large animal restraint and had proceeded accordingly.

There must be a higher power that watches over proceedings like this and gives grace to those who don't know what they're doing. Everyone came out just fine in the end, and I carried that stick around with me in my truck as a conversation piece for years.

As for the supremely un-conversational owner of Black Jack, he received the news of the stick in typical fashion. When the time came to send Black Jack home to his chicken coop, I revealed the true nature of the problem to the man. I gave him a brief synopsis of my surgical ministrations and concluded by dramatically pulling the stake out from behind my back.

He studied it for a few moments and said, "Oh, part of a fencepost." Then he loaded my patient in the livestock truck and disappeared down the road. I suspect that he must have been overwhelmed.

CHAPTER 12
Phone Sex

"Hello, Doctor. Thanks so much for returning my call. I just got home from work and my poor cat seems to have broken her back. I need to bring her in to the clinic immediately!" The caller was breathless and obviously in great distress.

It was early in the spring so I had trouble suppressing a little smile. "What has the cat been doing all day?" I asked.

"That's the strangest thing. She's strictly an indoor cat and hasn't ever been outside. She's in terrible pain, howling, and unable to use her front legs at all. Her hind legs work, but she just keeps her chest pressed down on the floor and screams. She's actually writhing in pain. I can see it!"

"Is your cat spayed?"

The owner is obviously perplexed by such a seemingly inconsequential detail. "No, not yet, we were just planning to call and make an appointment for it."

Now I relax and smugly pop my dinner into the preheated oven. This evening is going to be better than I had imagined a few moments ago.

I ask the caller if the cat is "treading" her hind legs and backing into inanimate (or sometimes animate!) objects.

The caller now probably thinks I have magical powers of perception.

"Why, actually she is. She's backed up against my rain boots right now, her hind paws are sort of marching, and she keeps twitching her tail. How did you know that?"

I try to be kind in breaking the news that their kitty is a grown cat now and exhibits all the traits of a female cat in full heat. When they see the process in that light, they are horrified not only that they missed the significance, but also because their sweet cat appears to them to be the queen harlot of all cats.

I assure them that all cats act this way and remind them that cats are one of the most reproductively successful species known to man. It should be obvious that this is one of their inborn agendas. It is merciful that these poor souls can remain relatively anonymous in their state of embarrassment.

***

"Hello, Doctor. I'm sorry to have to call you on a Sunday afternoon, but our dog is so sick that I really think she needs to come into the clinic right away. She's having terrible diarrhea."

I was familiar with the dog, a geriatric spaniel, and I started asking some history questions. My mind began to tick off the significance of what she was telling me with respect to an older patient. The caller quickly explained that she was inquiring about a new dog that they had adopted as an unwanted pet from an acquaintance recently. They had not yet brought this dog into the office. The dog had passed some very nasty diarrhea, and it was so sick that it insisted on hiding under her daughter's bed. The dog had not eaten since the previous day and would not even come out to drink.

I asked some more questions. Was the dog vomiting? She didn't think so, although she thought the dog might have eaten some of the children's crayons. I asked why she thought that had happened. She said that the diarrhea was so bright green that it looked like it was full of blue-green crayons. A light went on for me.

"Is this a female dog?" I asked.

It was.

"Is she spayed?"

There was a pause and then the caller said that she had assumed so.

"But you're not sure?"

She wasn't.

I sighed and asked the woman to get a flashlight and have a good look at the dog under the bed, bring her out, and check her.

The owner put down the phone and I waited. I heard scraping noises, a few murmurs, silence, and then a scream. "Oh my God! There's a puppy under there!"

Bingo.

The canine placenta is a unique thing. I don't know of anything else that ever issues from a dog's body that is so amazingly colored. It was a bit of a gamble, but I was almost sure that the dog was nesting with puppies under the bed, and I was delighted to be correct.

So the case of the female mother dog was solved. The embarrassed owners regrouped for their new role. We all had a laugh and I hoped they learned an interesting biologic factoid.

***

"Hello. I'd like to speak with Dr. Truelove. She is a female veterinarian, right?"

The staff informed the caller that I was, indeed, female but was currently on farm visits and unavailable. They asked if they could help her or if she wanted to speak with my associate.

"No! I'll just call back later," she snapped at the receptionist.

With no idea as to the nature of the call, this scenario was repeated several times. Each time she called, I was unavailable to speak with her, and each time she refused to state the nature of her inquiry or give a return phone number.

Eventually, she called when I was in the office, and I quickly gave her my attention. After a few pleasantries, she launched into her story. She informed me that her boyfriend had been diagnosed with gonorrhea. I immediately concluded that she had mistaken my field of expertise, and I had hoped to interrupt her before she revealed too much more. But she had obviously rehearsed what to say and she would not be deterred.

Finally, the crux of the matter was revealed. She explained that she had (as she delicately stated), "messed with" her boyfriend. This was no surprise for me; it was a pretty liberated time. Then the shocker. She informed me that she had also "messed with" her male Doberman Pinscher and needed to know if she could have given the dog gonorrhea.

This is not information I receive on a daily basis. To my credit, I did not gasp or say, "*You what?*" I tried to be my most professional self and told her in all honesty that I was not sure and would have to do some research on the topic. She thanked me for my help and said she would call back to hear my findings.

After putting the phone down, I stared at it for a long time. Besides the obvious surprise about her "different" lifestyle, I was thinking several other things. Was she not upset or curious about where the boyfriend got the infection or from whom? Was she not worried about her own health? The questions went on and on, but all I really needed to address was her genuine concern for her pet. This was probably the easiest element to handle and so that is all I did.

Delving into some antique references about gonorrhea, I was able to determine that the dog could only be a mechanical carrier of the organism but would not develop an infection himself. My end of this inquiry was over and a lot easier than what I envisioned my caller having in store for her.

***

The tiny dog was covered in green surgical drapes under the glare of the operating room lights. My assistant and I had grown very quiet. The only sound was the ironically steady beat of my patient's heart on the cardiac monitor. I had reached the conclusion that the internal injuries were too extensive for repair. A very large dog had attacked the poor little dog, and I had hoped to save its life. Unfortunately, this was not going to be possible, and although the valiant little heart continued to beat, I had made my decision. I would call and obtain permission from the owners to euthanize their pet without allowing him to waken from anesthesia.

By this time, we were into the early morning hours, dejected and exhausted. Cases such as these exact a tremendous emotional toll on the staff. Alone in the clinic, my technician and I quietly went about the task of cleaning up in order to be prepared for the next day's work. To our dismay, the phone rang.

The technician looked up at me. Normally, the phone would automatically be answered after a few rings by an answering service that would then signal my beeper if it were an emergency. I shrugged and said, "May as well answer it. If someone is calling at this hour it must be an emergency."

She answered the phone and asked if she could help the caller. I was distracted with writing up the previous record and lost in considering all the "what ifs" of the evening.

When the conversation had gone on for a few minutes, I looked up to see what was transpiring. My assistant was standing holding the phone. Her mouth was wide open, and her eyes the size of saucers. I hadn't heard her utter a word in quite awhile.

Finally, she quietly mumbled, "I'm going to have to ask the doctor about this," and put the caller on hold. Then she drew a deep breath. In a shaky voice, she announced that the person on the phone had just had anal sex with his dog. She stopped for a moment to let that bombshell sink in, and then she revealed the cause for his concern. In the aftermath, he had been thinking over his recent activity and was now worried that he might have contracted worms from his dog in the act. She raised her eyebrows and stared at me.

To say that we were both shifting emotional gears at a rapid rate is an understatement. A tiny portion of me wanted to laugh at this weird and unreasonable concern. Another part was disgusted at the entire concept. I really have no interest in what consenting adults do in private, but there was no way I would ever be convinced that this dog had any consent about what had occurred. The animal lover in me kicked in, and I was mad. I did not want to imagine any part of the scene or the plight of the dog.

What I told this person over the phone was heavily influenced by the fact that I had just been through an emotionally and physically draining ordeal with another pet. It was very late and my judgment was probably not on an even keel. I told him not to worry about the parasite issue, but that he should watch very carefully, because there was a definite risk that in ten to fourteen days his male member may wither up and die.

Sometimes the dark side just sneaks up and bites me.

The caller received this information without a word. There was a barely audible gulp and a click as the line disconnected.

CHAPTER 13
The Tractor Ride

It must have been a great party, but I hadn't made the guest list. At least I hadn't made the A-list and my present entry on the B-list was looking far from glamorous. I clung to my precarious perch and tried to ignore the fact that the hand I was using to stabilize myself was uncomfortably close to my host's bouncing buttocks. My Saturday night entertainment never seemed to conform to the expectations of the general population.

Earlier in the day, I had left the clinic with our large animal assistant, a short list of farm duties to attend to, and the prospect of returning in time for supper and maybe even a little television. My life had become an exercise in flexibility. Veterinarians, especially those dealing with farm animals, have no set hours of operation. We start when the calls come in and return home when the work is done. An uncommon day would be one in which each assignment had been checked off our "to do" list in the order it had been written and no new items had appeared. More often, the beeper interrupted the designated rounds, a neighbor stopped in requesting our services "as long as you're in the area," or one of the seemingly simple tasks went wrong and ended up as a day killer.

This open-ended time frame made planning for personal life endlessly frustrating. The only person who could fully understand and sympathize with this inability to conform to schedules was someone else who had done the same work.

Employed in a mixed practice in Connecticut, my schedule required me to work every other weekend. I would take small animal office calls until noon and then spend the afternoon on farm calls. This made life even more interesting, because small animal emergencies often interrupted my duties on the farm. The beeper was the bane of my existence, and I still have heart palpitations when I hear the disturbing bleat from anyone's machine. Nobody ever summons the veterinarian with good news on the beeper. It is always another tale of woe that means your workday will be a little (or a lot) longer.

I had left the clinic at noon, but as the day wore on chaos had reigned. Every time I thought I might be gaining control of my day, the beeper would interrupt, and I would hastily pack up and speed off in a new direction. When it was well past suppertime and the end seemed in sight, the beeper sounded one last time.

The call was from a dairy farm that was new to me. The owner had a cow that was down with milk fever. When a farmer refers to a cow being "down," he means that quite literally. The poor beast cannot rise. This occurs frequently after a dairy cow delivers a calf.

In the first few days, the production of milk is so sudden and exuberant that the cow's body has difficulty regulating its calcium levels. All her available calcium is pouring into lactation, sometimes at the expense of the cow's ability to survive. There is a minimum level of calcium in the blood necessary for muscle function. When the level falls lower than that, muscles cannot contract and the animal is unable to rise. Untreated, they become less responsive, can fall into a coma, and eventually die from respiratory arrest. These animals need immediate medical intervention. It was always one of my favorite conditions to treat because the result of correct treatment is so dramatic.

The treatment of milk fever is to return the calcium level to homeostasis in the bloodstream by intravenous infusion. The process looks simple in the hands of an experienced practitioner. The cow is invariably lying down when we arrive, head curled around toward her tail, and she's resting on her chest. If the cow is so far advanced in the process that she is lying on her side, she is very close to death and can easily inhale any rumen contents that flow back up her esophagus.

We quickly pull her up onto her sternum, put a halter on her head, and tie it to one of her hind legs to prevent her from flopping back down on her side. This sounds easy but it most definitely is not if only limited help is available. Dairy cows are not delicate little animals. They are blocky, heavy, and not very amenable to manipulation. This is when we hope the owner has several husky sons and maybe a few farm hands available. More often, it is the vet, the owner, and an assistant straining mightily to get the patient upright.

Once the cow is up on her chest with her head tied to her hind leg, the veterinarian performs the act that is the "make or break" performance for any farmer. We use a very large bore needle in the jugular vein to administer the solution. Every farmer has seen this ritual at some time. It is always expected that the doctor will grasp that big needle, bring the arm back, and with one dramatic flourish pop it into the jugular vein, a small fountain of venous blood issuing from the hub of the needle. Like a crowd following the course of a javelin thrower, all eyes are riveted on the instrument, conversation stops, and the intake of communal breath is audible. This one act will either win or lose the farmer's trust. Any hesitation or repeated attempt at entering the vein generates a discouraged sigh as the owner's faith seeps from him and drifts out the barn window. The now deflated man can only expect the worst. It is clear to him that some neophyte is in charge of his valuable cow and anything might happen beyond this point. Their minds are full of memories of, "Good ole Doc X, Y, or Z" who never missed a vein in his entire career. "Those were the days."

A long rubber tube is attached to the needle in the vein. The other end of the apparatus is attached to a large bottle of calcium solution that allows the liquid to run into the cow's vein at a rather rapid rate. This step also appears ludicrously simple and yet is fraught with peril. There definitely can be too much of a good thing. If the calcium is administered too quickly or too much is given, the cow's heart will fibrillate, and she will die—very quickly. This will really infuriate an owner and is to be avoided at all costs. If this should happen to a large animal veterinarian just once, before daylight, every bovine owner in the surrounding four counties will know what happened, and the vet's list of clients will dwindle dramatically. This is what I learned in school, and why I never lost respect for that calcium bottle. It brought death just as adroitly as it restored life.

Out on the farm, or in a field sometimes, how was one to monitor the calcium requirements? We had no mobile blood analyzers in those days, no traveling electrocardiograms. Furthermore, finances were a concern. Farmers are on such a tight profit margin that they cannot afford any extra frills. Food-animal veterinarians were forced to work by the seat of our pants—literally.

The usual scenario was that the farmer would hold the calcium bottle aloft as it drained by gravity. The veterinarian would stabilize the needle in the cow's jugular vein. Attempting to listen to the heart at the same time would require an impossible juggling act, requiring at least one more hand. Even though the animal is severely incapacitated, it still is cognizant and unhappy with its lot in life.

As the life-giving solution flows in, the cow comes back to reality and starts to strain against its bonds. How to monitor the heart without using more hands? The obvious and successful answer to this I learned from one of my professors. We were taught that immediately upon starting the flow of calcium we should step over and straddle our patient's chest. By resting lightly on her like a cowboy on a bucking bull, we could easily feel the heart beating against our legs. If we felt any irregularity in the rhythm, the calcium administration was to be stopped immediately, averting potential tragedy. It was simple, it was free, it worked, and it was actually pretty comfortable for the vet, who was usually expected to work in crouched, uncomfortable positions.

My assistant and I arrived at the farm and found it dark. There was no sign of life. Late on a Saturday evening, there is not apt to be much going on at a dairy barn, but we were expected and were concerned that nobody was attending our patient. Having no idea where to go, we waited. The cell phone had not been invented yet, and we certainly had no access to a pay phone, so we sat in the dark and waited. We started realizing how long it had been since we had eaten anything. Every crumb of junk food had long since disappeared from the front seat. We waited and listened to stereo stomach rumblings.

Just when I began to think that I should abandon my vigil and go home, I saw headlights bobbing and weaving through an adjacent field. Eventually, the headlights flooded the dooryard with light as a tractor came roaring into the driveway. I introduced myself to the driver and he informed me that my patient was out in a field some distance from the barn. He said that there was no way that my practice truck would be able to negotiate the path to the patient and that we would have to ride there on the back of the tractor.

Although I had never met this man before, as the conversation developed, it was becoming pretty apparent to me that Saturday night on this farm involved some partying and this fellow apparently had been the life of the party on this particular night. I began to wonder what could actually be wrong with the cow, as the owner's powers of observation and reasoning seemed a little questionable.

Considering the invitation to ride on the back of the tractor, we looked and realized he wasn't talking about a wagon on the back of the tractor. There was no cab on this particular tractor. We were both expected to ride balancing on the hitch! I offered to walk, but he informed me that it was too far, and we needed to get there fast or the cow would die. We hastily threw supplies and equipment together that I anticipated needing. I would have no access to anything in my truck once we reached the patient. I usually carried most of my equipment in two, very large grips, and a stainless steel bucket. We quickly consolidated the essentials into one grip, loaded the bucket, and mounted the tractor hitch.

Tractor hitches are not meant for passengers. They move side to side with the motion of the machine and have no solid braces to plant your feet. In fact, there really was only enough room for each of us to place one foot. We each did the best we could with the other foot when opportunity presented.

My assistant grabbed the heavy grip and I took the bucket. The only handhold was the back of the tractor seat. I dispensed with any concerns of decorum, latched onto that seat, and hoped my host didn't notice that he was partially sitting on my hand. I was fairly sure that his level of alcoholic bliss would be enough to make him oblivious.

What followed went down in my personal history as the tractor ride of a lifetime. We lurched out of the driveway at an inadvisable speed, shot down the road, and suddenly dived off the road where there was no apparent opening in the hedgerow. He was driving directly into a solid wall of raspberry bushes that were higher than the tractor. The thorny branches whipped and snapped at us, threatening to rip us from our precarious perch. There was no point trying to stop our driver, as we wouldn't have been heard over the roar of the diesel engine. He plunged on, his head and shoulders higher than our shoulders, and ignorant to our plight. The only way to hold on was by clinging against the driver's back. I did notice that the onslaught had diminished although we were still plowing through the hedges. I peeked back and realized that my chivalrous assistant was holding the grip out at arm's length using it to shield my body. I was grateful and touched by his gesture. The jolting, bouncing ride continued after we exited the raspberry bush gauntlet.

We drove at breakneck speed through a plowed field, over a rundown stone wall and eventually reached our patient.

The cow was indeed down and languishing under a large tree. Another partygoer attended, the driver's brother. They were both in high spirits and anxious for us to be done with our ministrations so they could get back to whatever they had been doing before they discovered this unfortunate cow.

Nobody had thought to bring a flashlight, so we worked in the blinding light of the tractor headlights. I could feel my retinas melting. After carefully examining the cow, I agreed that she had milk fever, and I prepared to quickly treat her and be on my way. Fortunately, we had brought a halter with us and restrained her in the usual head to tail fashion. I removed the bottle of calcium and realized that in my haste to consolidate grips, the tube apparatus had been left behind. There was no way either of us was going back for another round trip to the barn. I would have to improvise. In the grip, I did have two fairly large syringes. I leaned over to my assistant's ear and hissed that he should fill these syringes from the stock bottle and keep passing them to me, refilling them as I injected them manually into the cow's vein. This was not standard operating procedure, and I was not happy with it, but could see no other way around the situation. Meanwhile, insensible to my crisis, the brothers made inane small talk and waited to witness the big moment when I'd pop that needle in the cow's vein and show them what stuff I was made of.

Ready to attempt my sleight of hand with the syringes, I realized that the cow was turned toward the tractor, leaving the available jugular vein on the dark side of the cow. There was no way we could move the cow, and I shuddered to think of either of the boozy brothers moving the tractor in such close proximity to us. I found a tiny penlight in the grip, grasped it in my teeth, and got a dim illumination of the targeted jugular vein. Both brothers lurched over to view the moment of truth. The stars and planets were aligned for me that night. As my hand swooped down, there was an audible "thunk," and a fountain of blood issued forth.

Nodding with satisfaction and apparently uninterested in what would follow, the brothers ambled off and clambered up onto their tractor to wait. My assistant and I began frantically passing syringes back and forth, half-blinded by the tractor headlights. I wasn't able to assume my position on the cow's back to monitor her heart rate and still administer the calcium. This was a very worrisome situation. If I killed this cow, I couldn't imagine our ride (or flight) back to the barn.

Finally, I had administered what I felt was a prudent dose of calcium and the cow was definitely showing more signs of life. I decided to release her head and see if she could rise. Most cows are a little disoriented after experiencing milk fever. We usually give them a few minutes to clear their head, and then nudge them in the ribs to encourage them to stand.

Occasionally, a cow will come out of this situation mad and agitated. Unfortunately, that was how this cow responded. She wasn't just mad. She wanted to kill. She leaped up, bellowed, lowered her head, and started to charge us. My assistant and I ducked behind the tree, our only available refuge. She followed. She saw the grip open on the ground with equipment lying around it. Head down, she made quick work of all of it, flinging it about and grinding it into the dirt. The brothers watched the show from their perch on the tractor. It was a surreal scene in the alternating blinding headlights and deep dark shadows.

Nobody was killed, and nobody was maimed. Eventually, someone grabbed the end of the cow's halter rope and managed to contain her. We scraped up and scavenged all the equipment, stuffed it back into the bent and muddy grip and bucket. I don't even remember the tractor ride back. I know that it wasn't worse than the ride out to the field, and paled in comparison to our recent manifestation of the Pamplona running of the bulls.

Eventually, my assistant and I had everything back in the practice truck. While the good news was that the beeper was quiet, the bad news was that we were faced with hours of cleanup when we got back to the clinic. We had to be ready should another emergency call come in. We had absolutely no idea of the time, nor did we care. We were scratched all over from the raspberry bushes, covered with mud, and exhausted. As we got ready to drive out of the dark farmyard, we turned and looked at each other. And we laughed, and giggled, and snorted all the way back to the clinic.

That night I fell in love with my husband, who was my assistant on that wild tractor ride. An old tried and true recipe for romance and yet, I still fell for it.

CHAPTER 14
Good Deeds Seldom Go Unpunished

Certainly, this was not why I had gone to veterinary school. The cold moon shone down on the rutted field where we wielded our shovels. Enveloped in an eerie mist, we were exhausted and verging on desperation. Once we had accepted responsibility for this body, it was on our shoulders, literally. Where had I gone wrong?

A routine call had come in with a tearful request that I come out and euthanize the old family pony before the children returned home from school. I had been treating the pony for a chronic colic problem for some time. During his many years of life, the pony had experienced deterioration of his digestive system related to repeated; episodes of internal parasites. There was no more to do at this point to ameliorate his situation. The pony had been through enough and it was time for a humane end. The family had settled upon this point. I gladly agreed to come immediately.

The old pony left this life gratefully and with dignity that early spring morning. When I looked around for the expected hole or at least a backhoe waiting in readiness for the burial, nothing was in sight. Grief had clouded Dad's vision, and he hadn't thought about the ultimate resting place for their large pet.

I suggested he hire someone with heavy equipment to come in and dig a hole. This was out of the question, he had said, as their home was rented and the property owner wouldn't allow it. Then I remembered a local service that would pick up dead farm animals and gave the man the business card.

Arriving back at the clinic later in the day, I received a frantic call from the bereaved pony owner. The proprietor of the disposal service was in bed with a bad back. There was no way he could collect the pony. The school bus was due in an hour, and the couple wanted to spare the children from seeing their pony's lifeless body.

"Please, Doc. Help us get this pony out of here!"

This was a nice family. I really felt sorry for them and wanted to help in any way I could. Knowing I was possibly courting family discord, I offered to have my husband, John, pick up the dead pony in his truck for a small fee and we would bury it in the field of a local farmer who was a friend of ours.

This is where things got out of hand. It is also important to keep in mind that the fee was the princely sum of twenty dollars.

We put the pony in the pick-up truck and covered him with tarpaulins. As John drove out, the school bus rounded the corner. Perfect timing! I headed back to the clinic while John went to see our friendly farmer. The news was again bad. His backhoe was out of service; the hole would have to be dug by hand.

Meanwhile, back at the clinic, I was finishing office calls when my harried and disgusted husband arrived. After filling me in on the apparently unbury-able pony (still under the tarps in his truck and putting on mileage), we began to explore other pony disposal options.

We let our fingers do the walking through the Yellow Pages. Under the listing for Rendering Plants, we found a number and called it. When the phone was answered, John asked if they took dead ponies.

The inquiry was met with deafening silence, and then a horrified, "Do we take *what*?"

"Dead ponies," John replied.

At this point, the voice on the phone identified the establishment as that of a rather nice local restaurant and hung up on him. The listing for Restaurants began just under Rendering Plants, and I had slipped up a bit in reading across the column.

A little comic relief and then we continued with calls and more calls. It became apparent that this pony was going to have to go in the ground by the sweat of our brows. We didn't have the heart to call the owner and get the family upset with what was now our dilemma.

Scene Two takes place in the friendly farmer's field after dark. The two of us were struggling to dig the best hole we could. We often hear the phrase, "A body was found buried in a shallow grave." This took on new meaning for us in that field, which had only begun to thaw.

Hours later, it was clear that we were not going to be able to bury this pony.

Our thinking became more creative, nay, more desperate. Why not cut the pony up, put the pieces in grain sacks and dispose of it in the town dump? Not strictly legal by dump standards, but certainly it was all organic and nobody need ever be the wiser. Besides, this was before the days of rigorous recycling, and we weren't the least concerned that there were no tidy bins marked, Equine Offal.

With grain sacks in hand, we began the grisly task. We decided to harvest a few pathology specimens for educational purposes as long as we were at this macabre task. Things did not go well in the collection process, either. I had nicked the colon on the now well-bloated pony and had gas and fetid ingesta blasted in my face. The sight of my spouse collapsed in laughter hurt more than the physical insult.

There is no way to convey how much more difficult this job was in the execution than it had seemed in the conception. The number of grain sacks required and the logistics were beyond our worst nightmare. We labored in the misty blackness by the dim illumination of a lantern, a veritable scene from Dante's Inferno. Suddenly, to our horror, a flashlight beam appeared, bouncing across the field in our direction. Nobody but the farmer knew what we were doing.

It was a small town and I could imagine the gossip, the destruction of my career over this goodwill gesture turned into deception. There was no place to hide so we stood our ground and waited.

To our delight, two huge Labradors, followed closely by two friends of ours, appeared out of the dark on their evening walk. They were rational people who would believe and sympathize with us! Not only that, but the wife was a biology teacher. We quickly explained our mission to them. I had been working at removing the pony's head when they arrived.

"Oh great! We're doing the respiratory system next week. Could you let me have the larynx?" she asked.

What harm is there in furthering the cause of education? The corpse was already desecrated. I gave her the larynx and threw in the trachea as a bonus.

Eventually, our friends went home and our seemingly endless task was complete. The grain bags were incredibly heavy as we hoisted them into the back of the truck. It was near midnight as we pulled into the farmhouse where we rented a downstairs apartment. It was located on a little rise off a main road with the paved driveway leading straight up off the road. The worst was over. Our upstairs neighbors, who were gentle vegetarians, would never be the wiser, as John would leave at daylight to unload the bags when the dump opened. This was before political correctness required us to call it a landfill. We slept the sleep of the righteous.

Dawn came quickly, and John dressed and went out to his truck.

He was back in moments, pale and almost wordless. It had rained all night, soaking the grain bags and leaving a river of blood running from the bed of his pick-up all the way down the driveway and into the main road. I dressed and began hosing the bloody driveway as he left for the dump. Lady Macbeth DVM. It seemed the more I washed, the more I saw.

Cleanup complete, I decided what we really needed to greet a new day was a big breakfast. Wanting to put the episode behind me, I busied myself with coffee, eggs, bacon, and toast—a celebration. Time passed, but no John. Breakfast got cold, and I had to leave for work. Just as I was leaving, he appeared wearing blood-soaked coveralls. The usual setup at the dump allowed trucks to back up and push loads off into huge dumpsters. For unknown reasons, the new setup required the dumper to throw bags of trash up over the side of the dumpsters. John had to climb about ten feet up the side of the dumpster with each bag and drag it over the top.

But the pony was indeed finally gone.

For several days, I waited for repercussions from this event but none came. The last ironic twist came later. My biology teacher friend was eating lunch at her desk when a new teaching assistant came in and started to chat with her. Somehow, the conversation turned to owning horses and living in the country.

The new assistant recounted the story of a pony their family had for many years that had to be euthanized, but fortunately, the helpful veterinarian had been able to assist them by picking up the body and burying it in a beautiful farm field. Every time the family drove by that field, they were so happy that their dear pony would spend eternity in such a lovely spot.

My friend came close to needing a Heimlich maneuver as she focused on the cabinet over the woman's head where proudly displayed in a huge jug of formaldehyde was a large larynx and portion of a trachea.

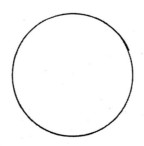

CHAPTER 15
The Joys of Academia

Seated in front of a college classroom I felt distinctly uneasy. Class members bent over their midterm examinations, scribbled furiously, and occasionally stopped to scratch their heads or flip pages.

Where was Ralph? Although he had one of the highest grade point averages in my class, he always managed to arrive for any scheduled test later than his classmates did. This was the most important exam I had given yet, and it had begun a full twenty minutes earlier.

Ralph would usually erupt through the door some minutes after his classmates had attacked their work, mumble an apology, grab his paperwork, and slide into a seat. He would then begin an agonizing process of test taking that involved swaying back and forth over his desk, scrubbing his hand through his hair, and making a noise sounding like a cross between groaning and humming. Then there was his left leg. As soon as he grasped his writing implement in his right hand, his left leg began a staccato rhythm of twitching vibrations as he alternated between bumping his knee on the bottom of the desk and bouncing his heel off the floor. Like an internal, single-stroke engine was driving the thought process from his brain down through his arm onto his paper, he motored on. It was annoying to everyone in the room, but several gentle attempts on my part to quiet him had proven fruitless. Eventually I had left him to what looked like a form of agony as he plowed through the written questions. His classmates had grown accepting of his compulsive habit and did their best to ignore him.

Despite his idiosyncrasies, Ralph was a conscientious student, and I couldn't imagine that he would miss such an important test. I was worried that he might have had some kind of accident. I began to pace. Rather than disturb the concentration of my class, I decided to walk out in the hall, hoping I would see Ralph flying toward the classroom in his usual disheveled state. I entered an empty hallway and began to walk.

As I neared the end of the hall, I sensed a low-pitched sound that was strangely familiar. As I got to the door to the stairwell, I knew exactly what it was. I eased the door open, crept to the top of the stairs, peeked down, and sure enough, there was my wayward student. He had his notes strewn about him, hovering over them as he rattled his leg, scrubbed his hair, and groan/hummed.

It would appear that he had calculated his "cram for the exam" time down to the last possible minute and would show up at class with just enough time to actually take the examination and be finished in time for the end of class. I had noted that he was always the last to leave, no matter how brief the test I was administering.

"Ralph!" I bellowed as the stairwell provided a satisfying reverberation. "Please collect yourself and get into the exam immediately."

Springing up and flapping his arms as he retrieved his paperwork, I couldn't help thinking he looked like a chicken that had just been scared off its nest. I was not particularly proud of myself but was delighted to have solved a little mystery.

Although veterinary medicine had been my all consuming goal and interest, there was always a nagging urge in the back of my mind to teach. I never expected to have a formal outlet for this aspiration, but I was presented with an intriguing possibility while working in Connecticut several years after graduating from veterinary college. The practice was close to Quinnipiac University and its highly esteemed veterinary technology program. Graduates often found employment in research and industry, which was the direction the curriculum had taken. However, there were also students who wanted a more clinical education, and there were no staff members with any clinical experience to share. Since many of the students planned to seek jobs in private veterinary practices upon graduation, the director of the program was looking for a practicing veterinarian to teach a few courses.

I had arranged a meeting to discuss the opening with the director. What he proposed as far as time commitment—one class given on two days of the week—seemed possible despite my daily obligations at the clinic. I would be teaching a class on Surgery, Radiology, and Anesthesiology for the Veterinary Technician. There was a textbook for the course, and I was sure I could teach the material on this level.

Before I allowed myself to be swept up in the idea, I discussed it with my employer, Dr. Arnie. I offered to take a salary reduction to make up for time that I would be away from the practice. The most I dared hope for was that he would grudgingly agree to my proposal. But, being the generous person that he was, he not only agreed to let me take the position, but also insisted that there would be no change in my salary. I made a mental note to try to emulate him if I ever had a clinic of my own. With great excitement, I called and accepted the position at Quinnipiac.

The situation for a neophyte teaching at university level could not have been more advantageous. The students were enthusiastic about hearing from someone in the real world, the subject matter was straightforward, and I always had fresh material from my daily practice. I fed off the energy of the students, and I felt we all had a great semester. I had fun making up challenging exams, and their performance was gratifying.

My course was only offered in the fall, so I was not sure what would happen when the spring semester began. It was obvious that the students wanted practical exposure and the school was satisfied with my performance, so I met with the director to discuss options. He threw out an idea for my consideration.

Years before, the program had offered a course on Light Horse Management geared toward giving students basic health, maintenance, and care information they might need to work with a large animal veterinarian, stable, or research facility that utilized horses. Would I be interested?

I couldn't believe my luck. This was right up my alley. There were only two problems. First, there were no existing notes or syllabus from the previous course, and no textbook had been used. More importantly, the college had no large animal facilities, and this was a laboratory class. Besides having lectures twice a week, there would have to be a two and a half hour laboratory session once a week to satisfy credit requirements. Having tasted the sweet fruit of teaching, I wasn't ready to back down. I plastered a confident grin on my face, shook the director's hand, and said, "No problem. I can do that."

On the ride home, I mulled over how I was *ever* going to do that.

Some frantic times followed as I desperately pieced together a curriculum and a sequence of lab sessions that would work with the lectures. I decided that the real world would be our laboratory. I would use my existing horse clients and their animals to demonstrate some of the principles. I made mental notes of situations and stables that would be appropriate and willing to cooperate. Every person I contacted was agreeable to allowing a class of twenty college students to participate in some kind of demonstration at their facilities. Again, I had to feel thankful for working with such great people.

This was New England, so it was important to consider the weather. I decided to hold the first few lab sessions indoors, realizing the students would not be prepared to be outdoors, or even in a stable, for several hours without freezing. I thought it would be important for them to have some hands-on experience with horse anatomy. Since most of the problems that horses have with their legs involve structures from the knees and hocks to the ground, I thought doing dissections of this area would be an excellent experience.

Normally, biological supply houses provide specimens for such dissections. The specimens, preserved in formalin, often have the veins and arteries injected with colored latex for easy identification. These are expensive. In retrospect, I realize that I had not even inquired about an expense allotment by the university for my class. I just assumed that I was on my own and decided to be creative in providing the class with material.

Fired by the clueless enthusiasm of my youth, my plan was to have the students dissect in pairs; half the class would dissect front legs and half the class would dissect hind legs. It would have been easier to have gotten just one leg and dissected it for them, but I wanted this to be a memorable experience, not a boring demonstration. The next blip on my radar screen was the fact that I did not have a source of legs. My macabre search was on.

John had a great idea. He knew of a slaughterhouse in our area, and he had heard that they processed horses for shipment to Canada. I cringed at the thought, but driven by the need to get my material, I rationalized that processing the poor animals would occur whether I collected the samples or not. Perhaps they would add something to the students' knowledge of horses in their passing. Since the legs contain no useable material, the slaughterhouse discarded them.

We made our call and learned which day of the week the slaughterhouse processed horses and where to find the discarded legs. We could come on that day and take as many legs as we wanted at no charge.

The collection day arrived, and I decided to wait until we were sure the process was over. I couldn't bear to witness the fate of the animals and hoped to distance myself as much as possible. I felt like a traitor having anything to do with the use of an equine for food, but tried to justify it on the basis that the wasted material provided an educational opportunity for my students.

We arrived late in the afternoon to find the facility deserted. We hesitantly searched for the described area and eventually found several metal barrels holding legs that had obviously come from ponies. On one hand, this was even sadder and more poignant, but on the other hand, my practical side was relieved that we would have smaller subject matter to transport.

We selected all the specimens we needed, and on impulse, took two skulls that were in the discard barrels, knowing that they would be useful in demonstrations later. Anxious to be out of this depressing environment, we loaded the legs and skulls into the bed of John's truck, covered them with a tarp, and headed for home.

On the way, we stopped at a convenience store for gas. The attendant came out and began fueling the truck. When the tank was full, we looked out the window to pay, but the attendant had disappeared into the store. We waited and waited for his return. When we were at the point of going to look for him, he came out, slowly rounded the back of the truck, and came to the driver's window to take the payment. He stared at us for an inordinate amount of time, and then returned to the store. We drove off without thinking anything more.

We arrived back at the clinic, unloaded our grisly treasure, and cleaned up the truck. After some minor trimming, I had the legs ready to go for my upcoming lab session, and I was feeling pretty good about it. The worst was over, or so I thought.

Two days later, John got an angry call from his older brother who worked for the local State Park Service. He had received a courtesy call from the game warden informing him that his younger brother had been reported for "jacking deer" out of season. Recognizing the name, the game warden had decided to alert John's brother before he arrested

John. Completely baffled, John assured his brother that this was not the case and asked who had reported it and on what basis.

"A gas station attendant saw the dead deer in the back of your truck the other day," he had said.

When John stopped laughing, he explained to his brother about the pony legs. It seemed that the tarp had been dislodged by the wind while driving, and the hooves must have been visible. Unfortunately, the man couldn't tell a single hoof from a cloven hoof, jumped to a conclusion, had written down the license plate, and turned it in to the state authorities.

John was about to be arrested for a good deed! The explanation was passed down the line to the game warden, and all went well with that lab session. In hindsight, I realize that I had chosen a very treacherous road for my spring semester endeavor.

Nothing from the fated trip to the slaughterhouse seemed to reside under a fortuitous sign.

After cleaning both skulls to the best of our ability, which entailed a great deal of work, we still needed to bleach them. Commercially, this is done in large vats with special solutions that whiten the bones making them more esthetically acceptable. We had no access to anything like this and so chose the old-fashioned route. When the weather got warm, we placed the skulls in the sun in a sheltered spot in our vegetable garden. We chose this remote spot to spare the upstairs tenants from any contact or awareness of our odd project. We lived on a well-traveled road, but the garden was hidden behind a wall of raspberry bushes and thus was sheltered.

After a long day at work and in class, we arrived home just in time to see a local neighborhood dog fleeing with its prize. Head held high, the dog was barely managing to move forward while dragging a pony skull between its front legs. Leaping from the car, we managed to salvage the second skull from the dog's cohorts that had gathered in the garden, drawn by this unexpected delicacy. We were never able to retrieve the other skull, and I had vague nightmares about the reaction it must have initiated when the dog dragged home its illicit treasure.

After studying the dissection of the leg, and lectures on function and lameness issues, the students were ready to see the knowledge put to use. I frequently visited a large boarding stable that had an indoor riding ring. One of my clients had called to have his horse's lameness treated. I felt this would be an ideal opportunity to pull all the information together. We arranged for the class to meet at the riding arena on the appointed day.

I took my patient from his stall and began walking him around in the arena. To evaluate the horse's soundness or lack thereof, it is customary to trot the animal. This accentuates the irregularity, and by analyzing the pattern of head bobbing associated with the trot, we are able to decide which leg is the problem. Occasionally, we can even localize it to a particular area of the leg.

I had the horse walked and then trotted, but I was not having success getting the students to see what was to me, an obvious lameness. On the verge of frustration, I realized that many of them had almost no experience with horses and may never have had an opportunity to observe a sound horse in action.

I quickly grabbed another lead rope and surveyed the long row of equine heads protruding from the open top half of their stall doors. For my demonstration, I needed a horse that was guaranteed sound, and that I knew well enough to put on a halter and take for a little jog around the arena. I settled on Broadway Joe, a delightful patient of mine that had recently been through an almost catastrophic siege of colic. We had ended up taking him to an equine specialty facility for emergency surgery. He and I had a lot of history together, and I had occasion to handle him many times. He was a sweet and cooperative gelding, well on his way to full health. He would be an ideal subject. I put on his halter, snapped on the lead, and led him out into the arena.

The students gathered and I reviewed what I wanted them to look for in the horse's gait. I walked Joe up to the end of the ring, clucked to him, tugged the lead shank, and started to trot off. A minor explosion ensued on the other end of the rope. My erstwhile placid patient seemingly levitated off the ground, and erupted into a swaggering, charging mass of battle steed.

Almost jerked off my feet, I struggled to stay with Joe. Neck grandly arched, nostrils flared, front legs pumping like pistons, and eyes flashing, he covered the length of the riding arena in no time. In the best of times, I am not a runner, and clad in rubber barn boots up to my knees I was more than a little handicapped. We stopped and turned. I was out of breath. I looked back at my expectant crowd. Maybe Joe had been spooked by the presence of so many people. What had happened to the Joe I knew so well? Surely, he would settle down. I decided to keep going.

But it was not to be. I'm sure that the conclusion most of my students drew in the end was that normal, sound horses dance, plunge, and do grand jeté movements through the air at great speed while lame horses merely trot along. I was exhausted, trembling, and grateful to have avoided being trampled under those flashing hooves.

I put Joe back in his stall while skewering him with my most unkind looks and mumbling a few unrepeatable words. As I slid the halter over his head, I had a flashback to the last progress report I had received from his surgery team where they mentioned that, to aid in his recovery, they had administered a potent anabolic steroid injection. These injections last for several months. They help increase appetite, speed healing and muscle development, and are very useful in such cases. They are also the substances used illegally in the body building industry and are very closely related to testosterone. I hadn't had poor old Joe out there on the lead rope; I had his evil alter ego, Joe the Stud Muffin that thought he was a stallion.

***

Our next session also involved another large riding facility with indoor arena. Actually, it was a posh show stable and had several indoor arenas for various purposes. The owner, in reality, had never really liked me very much. I had come to accept this. I had never done anything wrong to my knowledge; he just wanted to see Dr. Arnie whenever his horses needed care.

Dr. Arnie's personality was a better fit for him. He obviously had more experience, and the owner liked him to come when he made a call. When Dr. Arnie was not available and this client found that I would have to come out, a dejected sigh was inevitably his first response. As far as he was concerned, the B-team was on its way, and he would have to make the best of it. When I would arrive, he would repeat the exaggerated sigh, shrug his shoulders, and turn dejectedly to lead me to what he must have perceived as my victim.

I always worked very hard at that stable, more out of fear of fulfilling his expectations than because I had any wild hope of ever making him happy. I had chalked this account up to "you can't win them all" and did my best.

I hesitated to call this particular individual to ask if we could tour his stable for a class session. I fully expected him to turn me down, but it was such an excellent example of a large equine business that I thought it would be educational for the students. To my surprise, he quickly accepted. I actually repeated the request feeling that he must not have understood me. I must have flattered him enough that he seemed happy to exhibit and discuss the details of running a show stable with a class of college students. We set up an agreeable date.

Before the class met on location, I spent some time reviewing stable etiquette and decorum. I desperately did not want anyone to embarrass me at this stable. The students all nodded their understanding and we next met at the stable.

To my delight, we received a very thorough and interesting view of life in an equine business establishment. This stable specialized in showing fine American Saddlebred horses, both under saddle and in harness. These horses are high-strung, high-stepping beauties. Their show preparation is a science, and appearance must be in balance with performance. Myriad hours go into their grooming prior to their arrival in any show ring. We learned about feeding, from both a nutritional viewpoint and actual delivery of feed to such a large number of animals. When he covered show preparation, the owner brought out a selection of fake tails used to enhance the horses' own tails in the show ring. They are wigs for horses. Fortunately, at this point, his back was to the class as he demonstrated how these hair extenders were applied, because giggles began to erupt from the back row, which I had to squelch with some stern glares.

The grand finale of our tour was seeing a fine driving horse in action. The owner had harnessed a statuesque animal to a small, two-wheeled vehicle, not much bigger than a racing sulky. He discussed the different parts of the harness, types of driving classes, and other details of his craft. I was relaxing and enjoying the entire show; a spectator with no effort required on my part.

We moved into a small indoor arena where he proceeded to drive the horse around, showing off the various gaits the horse had, some of which were very fancy, indeed. The horse presented quite a sight with arched neck, full tail flowing, elegant high-stepping legs, and apparent effortless movement as he floated around the ring. Driver and vehicle flowed smoothly along behind him.

Finally, the owner stopped, answered questions from the students, and then, to my horror, announced that next Dr. Truelove would drive the horse for them. Although I had been around horses most of my life and had ridden all types on trails and in show rings and foxhunts, I had never driven a horse, much less a fine-tuned specimen like this one. I politely declined, but my tormentor would have none of it. I *was* going to have an outing in this rig or it appeared the class was not over.

With great trepidation, I climbed into the cart and imagined the vision of grace I presented in my green coveralls and barn boots. I took the reins and was handed the whip that I did not intend to use, but the owner informed me it was customary. Ready to move off and without thinking, I squeezed my legs together as though an imaginary horse located there would know to move. We stood rooted to the ground. This generated a smug look, and the owner informed me that I needed the whip to direct the horse to move off.

I swear I did no more than touch that horse's hip with the tip of the whip, but everything after that was more or less a blur. My recollection is of one of those carnival events where the daredevil motorcycle driver rides his motorcycle up the vertical sides of a cage. We flew around that ring, and it seemed to get smaller with every rotation. The more firmly I pulled back on the reins, the more galvanized the horse was to redouble his efforts. I was working my knees and heels in a frenzy to control my phantom riding horse. Occasionally, I would see in the blur around me, the frozen smile on the stable owner's face as he had his little joke on me.

As we careened around, tilting up on one wheel at each corner, tail slashing into my face, hocks and heels pumping inches from my eyes, I wondered if I would die in a spectacular crash, as the cart was threatening to flip. I wondered how far I might be dragged and was mightily ashamed that my class would have to witness it.

Finally, either the horse tired of the game or my arms went limp and he had nothing to pull against, but he grudgingly began to slow down. The one thing I am sure of is that it was no conscious effort on my part that affected the halt. Actually, when we were eventually slow enough to make it non-life threatening, the owner shot out his arm, grabbed the horse's bridle, and pulled him to a stop. I sprang from the seat as if my life depended on it, which I felt was true. My legs turned to rubber, my heart fibrillated, and I was rendered mute. Still the owner grinned. Never before and never after that did I ever see him come close to smiling in my presence. But on that one day, he really enjoyed himself.

***

The semester proceeded more smoothly as the weather became increasingly warm. We eventually arrived at the eve of our last lab session. I had something special planned. A client had a young stallion that she wanted me to geld. This procedure is routine, and I had done quite a number of them. I felt it would be an excellent chance for my class to observe general anesthesia in a horse as well as a routine surgical procedure.

We had a lovely day for the surgery and everybody arrived at the appointed time. I explained the procedure to the class. First, I would administer a dose of a potent pain medication intravenously that also sedated my patient. When he was clearly relaxed, another agent was given intravenously that anesthetized him long enough to complete the surgery. The horse would lie down quite naturally, one hind leg would be restrained out of my way, and I would castrate him using an instrument that simultaneously cut off the spermatic cord and crushed the blood vessels to stop any bleeding. This instrument was held in place for a few minutes and then removed. The horse's leg was released and shortly thereafter, he would awaken and stand up. They were usually a little groggy but calm, and often would even start to graze.

I administered the anesthetic and everything went right according to plan. I had warned the class that it was common to have a small amount of bleeding after the horse stood up. Unfortunately, this horse stood up and began to bleed more than a little bit. In fact, to my horrified eyes, it looked like a small hose was running. A pool of blood collected at my patient's feet. My face blanched, and I quickly caught eyes with my assistant, John. He looked pale as well. The class, all twenty or so, stood calmly by, obviously thinking this was what I meant by a little bleeding.

Time slowed. I searched through the instruments, found some surgical clamps, and made futile attempts to locate and stop the bleeding. All this seemed to do was disturb my patient that was intent on grazing and wanted to be left alone. I kept sidling next to John to have surreptitious, hastily whispered conferences. Neither of us had ever seen a horse bleed this much after being gelded. I tried packing gauze in the area, but still to no avail.

The worst part of the entire scene was the naive, calm looks on the faces of my assembled audience. I wished desperately that I could make them all disappear so I could have a proper panic attack. In desperation, I decided to make a hasty call to my employer to see if he had any words of wisdom for the occasion. I told John I would run up to the owner's house to use their telephone and asked him to hold down the fort. What did I think he could do when I had practically thrown up my hands? Feeling like a coward, I hastened off to the house.

After several frantic calls, I was unable to locate Dr. Arnie and returned to face my Donnybrook. I feared I might find my patient lying in a pool of his own blood, slowly expiring.

To my amazement, as I crested the top of the hill, I found the scene essentially unchanged but for one major item. The flow of blood had noticeably decreased. In fact, I could now describe it as a steady drip instead of a flow. John was looking a little better, too. The horse was taking advantage of his access to the lush grass and filling his belly. The class was looking restless and bored. I had just suffered a major professional meltdown, and they apparently didn't have a clue.

I quickly said a prayer to every entity that might have influenced this event and thanked my stars and planets. I pasted on a calm face, made a few more comments to the class, and then told them they were free to leave whenever they wished. When the bleeding had stopped, and I was sure that my patient was out of danger, we packed up and left.

The inside of the cab of my truck had never looked so wonderful to me. Once again, my supposedly well thought out laboratory session had turned into drama of epic proportions, at least from my viewpoint.

Looking back over the events in my class, I enjoyed it tremendously. However, I always wondered what the students had extracted from it. Attending a major veterinary continuing education program recently, I was reunited unexpectedly with one of the members of my class, now a practicing veterinarian herself. She informed me, to my delight that at least three of the students had gone on to graduate from veterinary colleges. If they weren't scared off by my demonstrations, I can at least say that I gave them ample warning that life as a veterinarian is not for the faint of heart.

CHAPTER 16
The Pawnshop

I gazed at the hunting rifle propped behind our big office safe. Like a moray eel, only the tip of the muzzle peeked up out of its lair. September was closing in on us, and I had good reason to believe the firearm would be gone soon. That would mean one more debt paid off, at least for the time being. There was no telling when we might see the owner of the leather ski pants, if ever.

Often, pet owners run into unexpected financial burdens—they become ill, have an accident, or some other calamity. When this happens, money is not immediately available to pay the vet bill. When the client has a longstanding history with the clinic, there is no problem extending goodwill credit. Other times, we are dealing with a new client or the owner is unsure when they may be able to pay the bill.

Four years of veterinary education had prepared me for a vast array of challenges. We learned the machinations of a multitude of animal species, their behavior, idiosyncrasies, and specific nutritional needs. We learned how anesthetic agents work, and the ways to troubleshoot a gas anesthetic machine. We learned federal laws concerning our use of narcotics and the international transportation of animals.

But where was that crucial class that explained accounts receivable and proper etiquette for reclaiming pawned items? Which professor forgot to tell me the niceties of storage for items that would not fit in my safe? I graduated without ever touching a firearm, not knowing that in a few years a rifle would be legal tender for my trade.

When John and I bought the clinic, it came with a strange little tradition. Vermonters are eminently practical, and old-time Yankees shun the use or even ownership of credit cards. The very idea of possessing a small, plastic entity that can lead to deeper debt is heinous to them.

The previous owners of the clinic had established a practice not unlike a pawnshop. If the bill could not be paid at the time of service or soon thereafter, they would permit the client to bring in an article of similar value, and it would be held at the hospital until the owner could pay off the bill. There was no interest charged and collection agencies did not come into the picture. It was clean, simple, and usually worked out well for both parties.

Keep in mind that this happened in rural Vermont in the early 1980s. ATMs weren't on every corner, and there was no Payday Loan. I can't imagine asking a client now if they wanted to drop off the family jewels until they were able to pay. But it was functional at the time and we decided to continue the practice.

***

My first experience with the pawnshop principle started after an emergency appointment treating a dog hit by a car. The owner, a distraught young man, rushed the dog in one evening. The dog had jumped out of the window of the moving car and been struck in midair by a vehicle traveling in the opposite direction. Injuries were fairly extensive, but eventually the dog was patched up and ready to go home. I had just started working in the clinic, and I was concerned when the fellow said he could not pay the bill. Feeling trapped in the cross fire, I sought out my employer.

I was a recent graduate, and I held Dr. Judy with her years of practical experience in great esteem. She seemed completely unflappable. In emergencies, she was cool and focused. Faced with situations that I had never even read about in a textbook, she would somehow figure out how to formulate a solution. And when it came to the financial end of our work, she was, She Who Must Be Obeyed.

I dared not discharge this patient without full payment. Therefore, clutching the record card, and with more than a little trepidation, I approached Dr. Judy. She glanced at the dog's documentation, studied the owner's name, and said, "Ask him if he's Keith's brother, and if he is, ask him if he has a hundred dollar gold piece."

Then she resumed what she had been doing. I stood with my mouth agape and several new questions on my mind. I figured I had missed some important class on client relations in school, but left the room to follow my orders like a good soldier. As it turned out, this *was* Keith's brother, and when asked about the gold coin, he thought for a moment then brightened up; he said he did have such a coin.

I returned to my employer with this odd tidbit of information. She said, "Fine, then tell him to bring it in, and we'll hold it until he can pay the bill. It will be in our safe."

Again, she resumed her work. Later, when my curiosity overcame me, I asked about the gold coin client. She told me that this family had created trust funds for their offspring who were living off the trusts at the time. Although they had access to considerable funds, the money was not speedily obtained or readily at hand.

The infamous Keith had a male cat that had recurrent bouts of urinary tract obstruction. This is an emergency and often results in large expenses. On several occasions, Keith had used the valuable hundred dollar gold piece, left to him by his parents, as collateral. My employer had correctly assumed that the parents had given each of their children such a coin.

This was also my first introduction to a Vermont phenomenon we call "trust fund hippies." This unique population of baby boomers came from wealthy families. They are usually very nice people who live quiet lives and have great respect for the environment. They made wonderful clients; they loved and collected pets, and were available for appointments at any hour of the day thanks to their lives of ease.

For many years, we would have one or the other brother's gold coin in our safe. They were lovely to look at and took up very little space. And they never failed, eventually, to be reclaimed.

***

Not every valuable was so well loved. Over the years, we had many, many items, usually of lesser value, that languished in our safe. We managed to accumulate boxes of inexpensive jewelry, turquoise, silver bracelets, and many rings. Most surprising were the number of wedding bands we held as collateral and the number never reclaimed. We could have provided the material for an interesting thesis paper for some sociology student or perhaps a romance novelist.

When the agreed-upon time for pick-up came and went, we would start calling and reminding the negligent owners. Sometimes we would find disconnected phones, sometimes people had moved. When it was obvious the item would not be claimed, we had to decide what its fate would be. A small attractive engagement ring was with us for years with no way to find the owner. I had it made into a pendant, which I fondly called the Deadbeat Diamond.

The inexpensive jewelry was fairly easy. At the clinic Christmas party each year we would put out all the unclaimed pieces and employees would draw numbers from a hat and choose a piece to take home.

Yes, jewelry was easy, but some of the other items were bizarre. Over the years, we held a pair of leather ski pants (à la Mick Jagger), a linoleum roller (this didn't go in the safe), a sewing machine, stereo systems, and much more.

One of John's favorites was a framed document signed by Samuel Adams. John is somewhat of an autograph collector and a history buff. He was salivating over the document, hoping that the owner would just leave town quietly and forget it. He took it out often to admire it. Days went by with no word from the owner and John's hopes grew. Then, on the morning of the last day he could claim it, the owner came in, paid his bill in full, and swept out with his prize. I was afraid John would chase him out the door making higher offers for it.

***

We also held many guns in lieu of bill payment. This is not odd in our area. Many people are hunters or own firearms. It was bad when a rifle was brought in to hold for a bill in the spring, because we knew the owner wouldn't have any use for it until hunting season opened in the fall. Sure enough, right before Opening Day, they would show up with the money and reclaim their weapon. Looking back now, I cannot imagine having a firearm in the clinic, but it seemed very normal at that time.

One situation had the potential to go very wrong. My associate went to the clinic on a Sunday afternoon to treat a dog that had an encounter with a porcupine. The dog's owner had never been to our clinic so we requested a deposit. He said he had no cash, and as it was Sunday, he couldn't go to the bank. This was before ATMs were so popular. He had no credit cards or checking account. When asked about items of value, he said he had a gun that he could leave with us as security. My associate agreed to that and met him at the clinic. After filling out the records, examining and admitting the porcupine-quilled dog, my associate went back to the counter. He asked the fellow for his gun, which the man slid across the counter. The scene was worthy of any barroom epic in the Old West.

Because my associate was a hunter himself, he was conscious of gun safety and thoughtfully asked the standard question, "Is it loaded?"

The man looked surprised and said, "Well, of course it is."

Dr. Steve slid the gun back across the counter and requested that he unload the revolver before handing it over. Just then, a police cruiser making customary Sunday rounds pulled into the parking lot.

The client, seeing the cruiser, shoved the gun back at Dr. Steve, and said, "Quick! Take this and hide it. I'm not supposed to have it."

Too shocked to do anything else, and thankful he had possession of the loaded weapon, Dr. Steve took it, unloaded it, and stashed it in the safe.

Just another day in the life of the country practitioner.

***

Probably the largest item we ever took in was a boat. A dog was brought in having trouble whelping. She was in very bad shape. Her uterus had ruptured, and she required immediate emergency surgery. She came through fine after much care and an extended hospital stay. The owner then said he couldn't pay the bill. Much discussion ensued between him and my husband about what to do about the bill. An agreement was reached, whereby we would have ownership of his boat until he paid the bill within a specified time. He lived in a neighboring town and John had seen the boat out on its trailer in the yard. The owner brought in the title and signed it over to John. Time came and went. The grace period had long since passed. We made many calls to the man's house. Most were not returned. After issuing ultimatums, John made a decision.

The clinic was quiet one day at lunchtime and John approached our associate who was rather large and of southern European descent. He asked him to accompany him on a quick trip during lunch. He said that the associate wouldn't have to say anything, just stand next to

John and keep his hands in his pockets (he happened to be wearing a trench coat). They got in John's pick-up truck and went to the boat's location, hooked up the trailer to his hitch, and prepared to leave. A woman came running from the house screaming at them to stop. John explained the circumstances, although she had been privy to many of the phone calls related to the boat and the payment. The showdown was about to take place as the two duelers assumed their positions.

"I'm calling the police!" she announced.

"Please do," John said.

Meanwhile, Dr. Trenchcoat stood over the scene and glared. He had clearly been in the drama club while in school.

The posse, in the guise of the police arrived. They heard the story, examined the title, and announced, "The man has got himself a boat." Then they left.

The woman had also called her husband, who suddenly realized he *could* pay the bill. He came home, paid in cash, and the trailer was unhooked from John's pick-up.

John drove off into the sunset a satisfied man. He hadn't really wanted the boat.

***

There were times when our financial negotiations resembled Bartertown rather than a pawnshop. Although Tina Turner never made an appearance in our version of *Thunderdome*, an exchange of services usually turned out to be advantageous to both parties. Sometimes it was the only way to be paid, and other times it was just more convenient for both parties.

Every time I snuggle under our cozy down comforter, I think of a tricolor English Cocker Spaniel trotting out our front door after having major surgery. Her owner had a small business that made goose down products. We wanted a down comforter, but we were on a limited budget as new business and homeowners and so were reluctant to purchase what constituted a frivolous extra to us. The client, faced with expensive surgery on one of his dogs, suggested that we exchange service for product. It sounded perfect, and indeed, it was.

We released the dog after surgery without the owner having to reach for his wallet. He gave us a voucher to use at his shop for the value of the service we had provided. On a free day, we made a pleasant trip north, picked up a wonderful quilt and some other small items, and all were happy. I could appreciate how it must have been during Colonial times.

***

A horse client in desperate straits, but with good intentions, had over time run up a sizeable bill with us. She had many animals but not enough financial resources to provide all that she would like for them. Her intentions were the best, and so we continued to let her charge various services. She would pay us what she could whenever possible. Her heart was definitely gold, but her aspirations were not within reach of her modest budget. By her appearance, it was clear that any money she had was going to the animals, not into her home or her clothing.

One day she approached me and told me how unhappy she was with such a bill hanging over her, though we had never complained. She asked if my husband and I could use any beef animals, as she had some cows that needed care and food.

We owned a small farm and had fencing in place, and so agreed to take two animals in exchange for her bill. I had imagined two, half-grown beef animals. What we got were a rangy underfed Scottish Highland bull calf and a slightly better looking Angus cross heifer. John saw their potential, but I was a little disappointed.

We wormed the pair and put them out on good pasture with extra grain and they blossomed. The bull was the extremely shaggy red type with enormous long horns. His pasture was located alongside the road where he got many visits and his picture taken by people who would stop by with their cameras. We named him Bruce Hornsby. Bruce and his woman had three calves over the years and more than paid back their worth.

***

Satellite Jack came into our lives at a most opportune time. He was a huge bear of a man who had spent a lot of time in Jamaica and had adopted the Rasta style of dreadlocks worn tucked up into a bulbous knit hat. Everything about him was oversized, even his beard. He was truly memorable and as kind and gentle as he was large. His big heart had embraced the Chow Chow breed of dogs and the family had accumulated what was classified as a kennel of these furry animals.

Jack had approached us about coming out to the kennel to update the dogs on their heartworm checks, vaccinations, and exams. After getting a quote for the service, he asked if there was any other way that he might pay the bill. I sent him to speak with my husband. To my delight, when they emerged from John's office, the men had huge smiles on their faces and shook hands at the door. I knew they had struck some kind of a deal.

John had asked what Jack did for work. At that point, John was prospecting for barter possibilities. Jack said he installed satellite dishes, and then in a burst of honesty he admitted, "Actually, I install black market dishes. I can rig them up and you get all the satellites without paying the companies."

We had recently moved to a slightly more remote location at the end of a long, dead-end dirt road. It was beautiful, but our kids found entertainment options lacking. There was no cable television supplied to our area. Satellite dishes were new and very expensive. We figured we needed an antenna from NASA to get anything but fuzzy reception on two channels.

John took this serendipity as a sign that we were meant to be part of Satellite Jack's outlaw enterprise. In no time at all, we had a dish and a staggering choice of entertainment. All of Jack's dogs were well vaccinated and checked out.

Of course, crime does not pay, and we quickly discovered a problem with our new entertainment. If the service is not sanctioned, there is no way to filter out any of the available offerings. Our children were young but quickly got the knack of cruising through the satellites, much to our (and their) horror. The number of X-rated shows was astounding on all levels. We needed to do something quickly.

We made an emergency call to Satellite Jack, who came out to the house one evening to fix the problem. The children were in bed, and he and John worked on screening and blocking sites. It was tedious and time-consuming work. Eventually, I got tired and went to bed.

I woke up sometime later. Where was John? I could still see a light in the living room and crept out to investigate. There was my husband, looking dwarfed in comparison to his companion in dreadlocks and knit hat, and both were sprawled on the floor flipping through porn site after porn site. Both looked half-asleep and miserable as they went through some sequence to block each signal. I couldn't help thinking how someone else might interpret this scene if he or she stumbled upon it. Finally, they had all the objectionable sites eliminated. Jack left and John fell into bed exhausted but glad to have that problem fixed—until the kids got up in the morning and found they could still get the full range of channels by using the remote control.

Today, we have almost universal use of credit cards, ATMs, Payday Loans and CareCredit, which eliminate excuses for being unable to pay a bill, even if the bill is unexpected. The human element is gone from the collection equation. Even though it was my least favorite part of my practice, there are times I really miss The Pawnshop.

CHAPTER 17
Pregnant Pauses

I stormed down the hall to John's office to break the news to him. I was exasperated. Not hesitating in the doorway, I swooped in and loudly announced, "That's *it*! The diaphragm is just *not working*!"

This outburst met with silence. John's expression changed from mild surprise to a silly smirk. Confused by his reaction, I finally took the time to look to my left to find one of our pharmaceutical representatives sitting quietly in a chair. He had been detailing some new veterinary products for John when I had made my entrance.

After my dramatic declaration, I noticed he was unable to take his eyes off my hugely pregnant belly. I had just possibly made the understatement of the century.

As Desi Arnaz often informed Lucy, "You've got some 'splainin' to do."

The clinic had one microscope that served heavy duty for the laboratory. Many staff members used the microscope and it suffered with the range of their abilities, or lack thereof. When it malfunctioned, we all felt its loss and hoped to have it returned to a normal function as quickly as possible. In most cases, John was able to put things right. As soon as a problem was identified, one of us would bring it to his attention, and we hoped in a short time all would be well again.

During one such period, the diaphragm, which opens and shuts to allow various amounts of light through the lenses, had been behaving erratically. This became more problematic as we attempted to use higher magnifications. I had mentioned this to John several times and every time he seemed to have corrected it, a new problem would arise.

I had just completed a challenging tumor removal, and I was anxious to get some idea of the exact nature of the mass I had excised. I quickly made some impression smears of it, stained them, and prepared to do a microscopic evaluation. Although these samples are ultimately sent off to a pathologist for diagnosis, we can often make tentative diagnoses right in our own laboratory. I focused on my specimen, increased magnification, and adjusted the light, but to no avail. Every time I focused in on an area of interest, the lighting would fade out, preventing any kind of examination. My frustrations mounted by the second that culminated in my inner office meltdown.

Having committed this incredibly embarrassing faux pas, the inevitable scarlet flush erupted from my collar and spread its glorious tone over my face. Unable to look either John or our pharmaceutical salesperson in the face, I focused on the far wall and tried to sound casual.

"The *microscope* diaphragm ... yes ... of course. Not working ... nope, not working at all ...." I threw my overstuffed body into reverse and fled the scene so they could have their laugh in private.

Before we purchased our clinic, both my husband and I worked for its previous owners. John assisted the husband with large animal calls, and I worked with the wife in the small animal clinic and did farm calls for horse work when it became available. During this time, we started seeing the donkey basketball team when they were in town. This was a mini-traveling road show that made their way around New

England. They were paid to come to fund-raisers to play basketball on the backs of donkeys. Usually a local group—fire fighters, teachers, or whomever—would be pitted against another group. The fun, of course, was to watch these hometown people, most of whom had never been astride anything livelier than a ride on lawn mower, try to stay aboard and jostle around the court to make a basket. The donkeys had the easy role. Clad in little rubber booties, they exercised their wisdom and agility by unceremoniously dumping riders at every opportunity.

When the group was in town, they used our facility for their motel. We worked out an arrangement whereby they would come in, I would tend to any medical needs that had arisen, and the donkeys would get some well-deserved R & R in our paddocks. The driver paid us a small fee for the overnight and was glad to have his charges out of their truck and happy. I saw anyone in need of vaccinations, health certificates, et cetera, when they arrived.

When I became pregnant with our first child, I limited my large animal work as the pregnancy progressed. During this time, donkey basketball appeared at our door looking for lodging and a few simple treatments. With difficulty, I squirmed into my familiar green coveralls. I could barely button the coveralls over my expanding belly, but knew that my patients were tractable little fellows and wouldn't require much from me physically.

The driver and I were well acquainted from several previous visits, and we got right to work. I checked one donkey's eye, cleaned up a small wound on another, and made out some health certificates. After finishing the paperwork, I went back to the small animal clinic.

Later in the afternoon, John came back from farm calls and went to the barn to restock some supplies. When he came back, he was very red and trying heroically to stifle his laughter. While he was working in the barn, the driver had struck up a conversation with him. After chatting for a few minutes, the driver had sidled over to him, lowered his voice, and said, "Did you see what happened to Doc?"

Concerned that I might have been injured working on the donkeys, John quickly asked, "What?"

The driver smirked, winked, and announced, "She went and got herself knocked up!"

There was a moment of silence as John tried to compose a response, then he settled on raised eyebrows as if this was news to him and a muttered, "Oh?" Then he left as quickly as possible.

***

In practice, I found myself particularly interested in the special problems and needs of performance dogs. These include hunting dogs, field trial dogs, Seeing Eye dogs, racing Greyhounds and agility dogs, among many others. I had joined an association of veterinarians with similar interests. During this time, representatives of the local greyhound track approached me. They were required to have a licensed veterinarian in attendance while the dogs weighed in as well as during all races in the event of an injury or question of health. Their long-time veterinarian was retiring and they needed someone to fill in until they could hire a full-time doctor. They had one local practitioner who was willing to take some of the days but couldn't work full-time due to his own clinic obligations. Would I be willing to work the remaining days? Although our clinic was busy, I felt I couldn't pass up a chance like this to work with some of the animals that so fascinated me. I didn't factor in that I was pregnant. I was still flying the flag of the invincible woman.

On my first day of work at the track, I arrived full of enthusiasm and more than a little concerned. This was out of my usual field, and I hoped I could learn quickly about the machinations of dog racing. Most of my responsibility happened behind the scenes. I would be present as each dog had its weight recorded and was then taken to a holding area for its upcoming race. When the trainer handed the dog over at the scale, an employee of the track then took over as the "lead-out." The lead-outs were almost exclusively young men. The job was extremely repetitious, and they found ways to make their days go more quickly. Some of their antics were amusing, others not so much.

When I was introduced in the paddock area, there were many long looks and a few nudges. They had never had a female veterinarian work at the track. I anticipated having to deal with a few rough spots but decided to see how things would go.

The work was easy and everybody was very helpful. I learned how to read the race card and eventually learned the insider slang they used. After a few days of work, it became clear that none of the lead-outs knew how to address me. It was a very informal bunch, and although they knew my given name, I'm sure they couldn't imagine calling me Dr. Stronk.

Finally, one of the enterprising young men dealt with the problem directly and announced to the assembled multitude, "So what are we going to call her? We always called the old vet 'Doc' and the other vet is 'New Doc,' so what are we going to call this one?"

There was general scratching of heads and rolling of eyes. I cringed to consider what they might consider appropriate and how I might respond to their choice. Eventually, a few pairs of eyes settled on my pregnant abdomen and someone yelled out, "I know … she's Baby Doc!" And so, for the years that I filled in at the track, regardless of my current reproductive status (and I did go through two pregnancies in that time span), I was known as Baby Doc.

I was fortunate in having a great, although nontraditional, support system. Whenever John and I faced childcare issues that required more hands than we could provide, my father-in-law would be on the spot at a moment's notice. He could be a short-order cook, was fearless in his approach to really nasty diapers, welcomed the challenge of a colicky baby, and had endless patience to sit and entertain the most persistent toddler. He had raised five children and now thoroughly enjoyed grandparenthood. His services were invaluable.

For reasons I never understood, none of my children would ever condescend to accept feeding from a baby bottle. They turned me into a virtual slave to their nursing schedules. With the birth of each baby, I would firmly state, "*This* one is going to accept a bottle." I was told it was critical to start the infant's exposure to the bottle at a young age. Everyone agreed on this point, and despite following every mother's magazine, pediatrician, midwife, or old maid's advice, none of my babies took a bottle on a reliable basis. I would eventually give in, decide we would both like each other better, and I would avoid gray hair if I just graciously ceded this particular battle. This presented many complications.

After the birth of my third child, I resumed working at the track on occasional weekends. By manipulating her feeding schedule to the maximum, I planned to feed our infant daughter just once during my shift at work. There was no facility for her at the track, of course, so it was time to call in my trusty father-in-law. He would come and stay with us on my track weekends, accompanying my husband with the three children to the track to meet me at my break time so I could nurse our daughter.

Our son was five years old and our other daughter was eighteen months old. The men could watch over the other children while I hid in the back of our van and nursed the baby. Most nights this worked out just fine. Other times it was challenging.

I never felt comfortable hiding behind the tinted back windows of the van, although my daughter was blissfully unaware. On one summer night, outside the vehicle, I could see my father-in-law giving our toddler a cup with some ice. I had asked him before not to give her ice, but he had raised more children than I had, and he had his own opinions on the subject. Suddenly there was a flurry of activity, he called to my husband and to my horror, they began shaking the child upside down, trying to remove an ice cube that was choking her. Unsupervised, my son started to wander off into the parking lot on his own as his father and grandfather wrestled with the wayward cube. Before I was able to react, the ice cube dislodged, our wandering son was retrieved, and normalcy (for us) resumed. The entire incident was over in a few seconds, I'm sure, but it seemed an eternity to me. Meanwhile, the infant firmly affixed to my breast was smiling contentedly. When I finally finished and wobbled off to the paddocks on shaking legs, I couldn't help wondering if Doc and New Doc had ever had such an adrenaline-packed work shift. The liberated woman thing was not all I had sometimes envisioned.

***

One would think that the clients are the only individuals who contrive to destroy a well- planned day, but sometimes the disruption started in my own gene pool. When my middle child was born, I made it my mission to convince her that taking an occasional bottle-feeding was acceptable. Indeed, we made great headway as the time grew nearer for me to return to work. Once a day, I successfully fed her from a bottle, and felt I had overcome a significant obstacle. On the first day back at work, everything went like clockwork. Our caregiver, who lived in our home at the time, was able to feed my daughter a midday bottle, and we anticipated a much smoother schedule for me.

On my second day back at work, I had scheduled a rather long and difficult orthopedic surgery. We anesthetized and prepared the Golden Retriever's leg. I did my own surgical prep. This included full cap, mask, and gown as well as a ten-minute scrub and gloves. My technician opened my surgery packs, and I carefully placed the sterile drapes. As I picked up my scalpel and prepared to make my incision, John entered the room looking apologetic.

"The babysitter is on the phone and there is a slight problem. Joy (our daughter) absolutely refuses the bottle and is screaming hysterically. She has been trying everything to calm her down but is having no success. Now they're both upset."

What to do?

After a brief conclave during which, hands held aloft, I maintained my surgical sterility, we decided that John would drive home, bring Joy to the clinic, and see if he had any more luck with her than the sitter had. At least she would be with me so I could feed her as soon as possible. I anticipated the surgery to take as long as two hours and figured that she would be extremely hungry by that time.

John left and I turned to view my sleeping patient, anesthetic machine whooshing and beeping, green drapes hiding most of his body. I took a deep breath to focus myself and made myself say, "No pressure." Yeah. Right.

I was well into my procedure when John appeared cradling Joy. True to her name, she was now smiling benevolently and seemed completely content. John looked apologetic but confirmed that when he arrived at the house the sitter had been so desperate to calm the child that she had resorted to the old stroller routine, pushing her in circles around the front yard. The rocking motion of the stroller usually guaranteed that a nap would ensue. Yet, she had been in full cry the whole time.

Now calm, it appeared that Joy would manage to hang on for a while before being fed, so I continued my work. Realizing that John couldn't just stand there holding her, we opted for a tried and true solution. John quickly went downstairs and retrieved our old trusty, rusty wind-up baby swing. This item was so invaluable that we had one at home and another at work.

Placed in the swing, Joy still seemed delighted. John wound the mechanism to its maximum capacity and started her swinging. Peace and quiet reigned. I expected her to tire quickly of this, but she proved me wrong. Neither did she drift off to sleep, which was an expected outcome. And so my operation progressed with me calling out requests of my technician, "More sponges," "Adjust the light please," "I need another clamp," "Rewind the swing," and so on.

Joy watched with intent interest through the entire operation. At first I was relieved, but later I became perturbed. If she had been that hungry, how did she just turn it off? If she demanded my physical presence, how could she even tell it was I? All that was visible between cap and mask were my eyes.

The surgery went well. We turned off the anesthetic, I quickly removed the surgical drapes, and we moved my patient into recovery. I yanked off my cap and mask, and took Joy to a private place to feed her, fearing she must be ravenous. But Joy would have the last laugh. When offered, she looked me right in the eyes, gave me her biggest grin, and dawdled as much as possible, giving me a clear message that she may be only a few months old, but she definitely had the whip hand in our situation. Apparently, she felt a need for some quality time with her mom and would not be denied. Interestingly, she is now the only one of my three children who can stand the sight of blood or surgery. Maybe children just need to be exposed at a young age.

CHAPTER 18
Unusual Requests

My mind was not clear after roused from a deep sleep, and yet, I was positive that I had nothing to say to a guinea pig on the telephone at 2:00 AM. Why did it seem that some of my clients were recipients of messages from outer space, and why did they feel that I was a logical person to consult on these issues? Reminding myself of my vow to remain respectful and honor any client request, no matter how bizarre, as long as it was legal, ethical, or humane, I made my decision.

Although most of us do see guinea pigs in the course of our work, it is usually the classroom mascot that is farmed out for the summer, or a pet that spends its entire life confined to its cage in some child's bedroom. For many years, I had a client deeply attached to her guinea pigs. The bond she shared with them was comparable to any devoted dog or cat owner. The first time I met the woman, I was on emergency duty. My beeper awoke me at 2:00 AM bringing a message about "a choking guinea pig." Confused, I imagined that it was a miscommunication, but promptly returned the call to the indicated phone number.

A woman who sounded wide-awake and very alarmed answered

the phone immediately. Her pet guinea pig was choking, and she feared that its life was at risk. I squelched my inclination to ask what in the world she was doing checking on a pet guinea pig at that hour. Still sleepy and unfocused, I asked some general background questions concerning the animal's age, previous health condition, living situation, etc. Although the woman answered promptly, I sensed her urgency; she wanted me to move along. The guinea pig had been fine up until that evening when it had started to choke, and the choking was getting worse. She thought her pet was having trouble breathing.

I toyed with the idea of scaling down the Heimlich maneuver and walking her through it on the phone. I resisted that devious urge and continued to question her. Never having heard any noise from a guinea pig other than squeals of protest during my examinations, I couldn't imagine what she was hearing. This was a very astute woman, and she quickly guessed ahead to where I was heading with my line of questioning.

I sounded a little skeptical about what she thought was choking, so she suddenly blurted out, "Here, I'll put him up to the phone and you can hear for yourself!"

The mental image of this woman in the middle of the night holding up a quarter of a pound of rodent to the mouthpiece of the phone so that we could communicate was more than I could bear.

"No no no!" I said. "If you think he needs to be seen, I'll meet you at my clinic in twenty minutes."

Greatly relieved, she said she would meet me there.

We arrived at the clinic together. As I opened the front door, she was a vision before me. A middle-aged woman in bathrobe and slippers stood cradling a little bundle. She almost pushed me aside in her haste to get her pet into the examination room. I spread a towel on the table and started to check out my new patient. I quickly saw that "Bart," as he had been introduced to me by this time, had very enlarged lymph nodes around his throat. They were large enough to be compressing his pharynx and making him sound as if he were choking. It was difficult to tell which of us was more delighted, the owner because she had her concerns justified, or me because I had an actual diagnosis.

I quickly made up a liquid antibiotic and administered the first dose. I instructed her on proper dosing and follow-up, and looked forward to rushing home and being back in bed for a few more hours of sleep.

As I ushered her out, the woman asked me to wait while she went out to her car. This was a little odd, but definitely not out of keeping with the way this night was going, so I obliged. She came scuffling back in her slippers and handed me a long package wrapped in tissue.

"This is for you," she said. "I was sure that anyone I called would just laugh at me and say that a guinea pig wasn't worth being seen as an emergency, and I appreciate the fact that you took me seriously."

Without further explanation, she scuffled out the door. In the package were two lovely hand-dipped candles. I wasn't really sure how this gift tied in with the evening, but it was a very nice gesture. How many of us have a little hostess gift at our fingertips at 2:00 AM anyway?

***

My professional relationship with the guinea pig owner continued over many years. During the course of time, I learned she was involved in a business that promoted the use of magnets for various health issues. She often touted the benefits and gave examples of how to use the magnets. I am open-minded to alternative therapies and always listened to her discourses. She sold me little quilted blankets with magnets so that I could use them to wrap up small surgical patients to aid in their recovery postoperatively. I could see no harm in this and was happy to try the magnets. Over time, we cease to notice that some people are perhaps a bit more eccentric than the general population.

They certainly can be more entertaining than many, and I found it easy to honor her requests. In retrospect, I see that daily life would have lacked much flair without these individuals. During one visit, she noticed that I was moving gingerly and asked me about it. I told her my back was bothering me, and before she left, I had magnets in the soles of my shoes

It transpired that one of the elderly guinea pigs under her care needed to undergo a surgical procedure. The owner was understandably worried about the risks of anesthesia. I shared her concern but said we would do everything we could to support him and anticipate any problems that we could. She was most concerned about his anesthetic recovery period and requested that she tend to him during that time. I was sure that nobody was more familiar with that animal than this woman was, and agreed that I would hand him over (wrapped in one of her magnetized blankets, of course) and allow her to hold him and comfort him as he awoke.

The surgery went well. As soon as I felt comfortable having the patient out of my sight, I wrapped him in the little blanket and had a technician take him to the owner in the waiting room. I had instructed her to stay there with him until he was awake and I authorized his release. I didn't think much about this as I continued to work on various patients in the treatment area. Some time later, a receptionist came back and asked if we could send the guinea pig owner home as she was freaking out the clients passing through the waiting room. She was such a quiet, introverted person that I could not imagine how she might offend anyone.

"Come see for yourself," the receptionist said.

I went to the waiting room, pushed open the door, and realized what she meant. There was the owner with the guinea pig cradled on his back in the blanket between her knees. His four tiny paws poked up in the air and his two prominent yellow front teeth grinned at nothing in particular. In each hand, the owner had a string attached to a ball about the size of a Ping-Pong ball. As she kept up a very quiet monologue with the awakening guinea pig, she was slowly swinging the balls in opposite directions in circles over his belly. It was obvious to me that this was one of her magnet deals, but I'm sure to others it must have looked like some voodoo ritual complete with incantations.

When she saw my face at the door, she looked up, smiled, and said, "He's doing great, he's almost awake. The magnets have done the trick."

Although I suspected that modern medicine had something to do with his successful recovery, I made no mention of it. I quickly checked my patient and told her it was definitely time to take him home.

***

Many of our unusual requests occur at the end of a pet's life. I strongly believe I can help in the process of losing or mourning a pet. I believe the real art of veterinary medicine is something we learn from experience. If you haven't learned to be a compassionate human being at your mother's knee, no amount of university education will prepare you for what people need when faced with the end of a beloved pet's life. Some people are comforted by routines that are not generally appealing.

It is often healing for owners to bury their pet or its ashes. Some will have some kind of ceremony for family or friends to mark the pet's passing, usually in the privacy of the home, but sometimes it spills over into our domain.

We received a call from a woman who was new to the area. Her aged Irish Setter had many health issues, and she realized the time had come to let him leave humanely. She asked if she could bring a blanket and be present in the room to comfort him as we euthanized the old dog. This is common practice, and I said I would be more than glad to accommodate her. She appeared at the appointed time and we showed her into the room. Physically, she was the epitome of the beautiful

Irish lass with flaming red hair and a fair freckled face. She wore a long skirt and boots and had a beautiful wool shawl over her shoulders.

Her companion was obviously the geriatric remains of what had been a truly grand old setter. He was tall, very angular, and shuffled his feet as he walked. His dark mahogany coat still sported long, well kept "feathers" down the backs of his legs and along his underbelly. He retained the aura of his former glory. But his eyes were his most striking attribute. They were sad and quiet and seemed to be looking into a place none of us was capable of seeing.

The woman brought a large canvas tote bag with her and asked if I minded if she had a few moments alone with her old friend. I said this was no problem and that she should just signal us when she was ready. As I was walking out, she made one more request. Would I mind if she played some music during the procedure? Of course not, I replied.

Time passed and eventually she was ready. Bringing a technician with me, I entered my exam room and found it transformed. In the corner was a large boom box playing heartrending music that I guessed was some kind of Irish dirge. The lights were off and the exam table was moved back from the center of the room. Several large aromatic candles flickered from the counter and corners of the room. Center stage was our patient, resting comfortably on a beautiful wool blanket that matched the owner's shawl. This was going to be a proper funeral for the old man.

The actual process went fine, although I was desperately in need of more light than was offered by the candles when the time came to obtain a vein to inject the solution. We all sprawled out on the floor for the process with our patient. I had an eerie feeling that Celtic spirits had visited us and swept the setter off to a strange place. It was extremely emotional for my technician and me, as we had stepped out of our usual professional comfort zone and been thrust into a highly personal event. Although we had never even met the owner or the dog before, we were filled with the loss that was occurring. We were having a hard time stifling sobs, shaking, quickly wiping at our dripping eyes and noses as we finished our task.

The owner, who had obviously put a great deal of planning into what had transpired, was clearly comforted. She alone was clear-eyed and occasionally quietly hummed with the music. When all was done, she repacked her things, thanked us very much for our efforts, and left. My technician and I were at a loss as to how we would resume normal function for the day, and have always had a sneaky suspicion that we may have had a brief trip to the twilight zone.

***

Losing a pet unexpectedly can be tragic, leaving owners no time for preparation. One of my clients had the great misfortune of having her little shaggy dog hit by a car and instantly killed. The family rushed the dog into the clinic to confirm their fear that it was beyond help. I spent some time with them in the exam room, discussed how unfair the situation was, and acknowledged their sudden loss. When the family had time to ask questions and come to grips with the situation, we ascertained that they wanted us to cremate their pet. Before I left with the dog, they had one more request. They wanted to take some last photographs of their beloved dog.

Although they'd had the foresight to bring a camera with them, I did not think this was a good idea. Unfortunately, one of his eyes was pushed out of its socket by the force of the impact. This is a grotesque image and never fails to make me think of the old cartoons where characters' eyes pop in and out of their sockets in surprise. In real life, this situation is never funny, and the eye does not return to its normal placement without surgery. I gently tried to dissuade them and encouraged them to remember their beloved pet as he was in life.

They would have none of it; they wanted one last picture. I cleaned up any trace of blood for the photo shoot and suggested that they lay him on his side with only the good eye showing. They proceeded accordingly.

My loyal clients had one more little request. It was important for them to have a photo of their pet in the arms of his favorite veterinarian. My heart sank. Just what I needed for good public relations—a color photo of me cradling a dead dog with its eye out of the socket and passed around for all to see. Although I appreciated their intent as a compliment to my care, this went beyond macabre. What was I supposed to do? Smile for the camera? What facial expression is appropriate for this event?

I know it is second nature for everyone to smile for a camera, and I was sure that no matter how much planning I did, I'd smile at the last minute out of habit. Thinking quickly, I seized the day. I gently picked up their deceased and cradled him against my chest, being very careful to turn his head toward me so the damaged eye did not show. Then I told them to move in for a very close-up shot. Fiendishly, I knew my motive was to eliminate my mug from this shot, and I kept coaxing them closer and closer before the shutter clicked. Eventually, I knew that they were close enough so there was no way my face was visible. I gave them plenty of time to get all the pictures they wanted, and I felt satisfied with my clever solution to this sticky problem.

Finally, they were done, but as I went to replace the body on the table I realized, to my horror, that his little head had been cradled on my chest directly under my name tag that stated in big bold print: ROBIN T. STRONK, DVM. No secrets here.

***

Very rarely an unusual request falls in a gray zone. This is especially tricky when the request involves the death of a pet and the owner's emotional needs during that time. A woman called to ask about our cremation services. Her daughter's dog had died and they were planning to have it cremated. They wanted to have an individual cremation and be sure that they received only their pet's ashes back. This is a common and understandable question. Then the line of questioning left the usual tract. The woman needed to know what temperature the crematory reached and the volume of the remaining ashes.

When asked why she needed this information, she stated, "Because my daughter wants to eat the cremains so that her dog will always be with her."

Although legal, ethical, and humane, this seemed to fall in the category of unhygienic. And in fact, the dog would not always be with her, but about as long as one cycle through the gastrointestinal tract. This was one request we managed to decline politely.

CHAPTER 19
I'm Sorry ... So Sorry

The hour was extremely late and prospects were grim, but the cardiac monitor continued to emit its reassuring "lub dub." I began to allow myself to imagine that our patient may possibly pull through this ordeal. Looking up at Dr. Dan, who was now in his second full day of veterinary practice, I was surprised to see him looking quite despondent. Dan had come to us directly out of school, and I was doing my best to mentor him. The new graduates could be challenging, requiring the energy of a Border Collie to oversee them as they made their initial forays into the practical aspect of veterinary medicine. My goal was to nurture these individuals, encourage their growth, and help them to understand what had happened when problems arose.

There was no other way to describe Dan but as a big teddy bear, an overused description, but there are no other words to explain him. The other adjective worthy of my new associate was hapless. Unfortunately, just like a bear lumbering on hind legs, Dan lacked a certain amount of grace. "Oops" was deeply ingrained in his being.

His first week at the clinic, Dan arrived in the morning looking embarrassed, and he presented the beeper, our answering service's contact with us, in many small pieces. While on emergency duty, whoever was on call kept the beeper clipped to their belt. Dan had fallen down and broken the beeper. There was no accident or exciting story behind it; Dan had just taken a tumble. Wondering if our young vet was going to need a walker by the end of his first year with us, we had the instrument replaced.

Dan was a hard worker and strove to be thorough. He was certainly uncomplaining. It seemed no matter how hard he tried to complete a given task, small details tended to go amok. One Monday morning, I walked into the treatment area and my nostrils were assailed by the heavy odor of cod liver oil. I asked if anyone knew where the smell was coming from but nobody seemed to know. This smell lingered for days and remained a mystery. Eventually, I had a feline patient I was working on that needed a dose of thyroid medication (Tapazole). This is a commonly used human drug available only in pill form, but cats can be difficult to administer pills to on a daily basis. We had found a compounding pharmacy that would put the medication in a liquid form and flavor it in any way we wanted. We quickly eliminated the bubble gum and orange options, but found that they offered a tuna fish flavor that fit our needs perfectly.

Since we used the drug so frequently, we decided to splurge and buy a large bottle of the medication to have on hand at the clinic. We had recently purchased a pint that had cost several hundred dollars. I went to retrieve the bottle from a shelf but was unable to find it. After thoroughly scouting the entire clinic, I still could not find the drug. Suddenly, the proverbial light went on in my head. The mystery smell had started after a weekend that Dan was working as the only doctor on duty.

I found a private moment with Dan and asked, "So Dan, how did the bottle of Tapazole get broken, anyway?"

His look was somewhere between relief and surprise. He had

actually hoped that nobody would notice. It was not that he was dishonest, just mortified by his clumsiness. Then he told the story.

He had a patient on Saturday morning that was very difficult to handle. He had carefully measured out the amount of the fish oil based medication that he needed, put the stock bottle down on the treatment table, and then proceeded to administer the dose. Apparently, this cat was less impressed with the tuna flavor than most. She proceeded to morph into a whirling Tasmanian Devil. In the fracas that ensued, she managed to fling the bottle off the table and it exploded on the floor. No matter how hard he scrubbed, Dan couldn't rid the room of the strong fishy smell. I told him it was an honest accident and hoped he would remember to put breakables out of harm's way when restraining pets. Even today, when the weather gets humid, I get an occasional whiff of tuna fish in the treatment room and smile when I think of Dan.

His worst accident happened after he had been with us about a year. He called in one morning when he should have already been at work to say that he would be a little late. When asked why, he stated that a car had struck him. He wasn't in a car accident; a car had actually struck his body. We were horrified. When he finally told the entire story, it was truly amazing.

Dan owned a large dog that was completely blind. They had a wonderful rapport, and he often trusted her to walk with him without a leash. He had the dog out for her morning walk in town and she suddenly darted off and ran away from him. They were in a busy area of town and he was frantic that a vehicle might strike her.

The good news was that the blind dog made it through traffic unscathed; the bad news was that Dan did not. Hit by a car, he was thrown up onto the hood. In his words, "Just like in the movies." Fortunately, he was only badly bruised. He insisted on coming into work as soon as the emergency room released him, although we encouraged him to go home.

When he showed up, he looked like he had gone a couple of rounds with a pretty good boxer. One eye was swollen shut, there was a sutured gash on his forehead, and every minute a new color of the rainbow appeared on his cheek. I again encouraged him to go home. Still high and impervious to pain from the monstrous adrenaline rush he must have experienced, he persevered and stayed. The last straw was when I saw the look on the face of a client who was about to be closed into an examination room with "rock 'em, sock 'em" Doctor Dan. The poor woman looked terrified.

As soon as he finished that appointment, I called him aside and said, "Dan, you have to go home now. You're scaring the clients." At last, he agreed, but it was a measure of his fortitude that he tried so hard.

My most endearing memory of Dan was when he had just started working for us and was on his first night of emergency duty. When we have new graduates, I tell them I will back them up on emergencies until they feel comfortable. This way, they get the experience of receiving the calls, doing the interviewing and selection or triage on the phone, and they can attend to the case on their own if they feel it is within their capabilities. If they realize the case is more complicated than they can handle, I am only a phone call away and come in to help.

Dan had an excellent grasp of his limitations. This was actually a good thing. It is much worse when the neophyte feels he or she can take on the world and ends up with a big problem that is difficult to resolve. I did not worry about Dan. He would not overstep his level of experience.

I was barely done with supper when the phone rang. It was Dan and he was falling over himself with apologies for calling me. As luck would have it, or certainly the "luck of Dan," his very first emergency call was the most dreaded emergency that a small animal practitioner sees—a dog with a gastric torsion. We see this swiftly advancing, life-threatening situation in large breeds of dogs. The stomach fills with air and becomes buoyant, and then it rolls over on its long axis, thereby cutting off its own blood supply. The contents of the stomach continue to ferment, producing more gas and dilating the stomach more and more, stretching the walls.

Meanwhile, the circulatory system is going into shock, and the dog is dying minute by minute. Unobserved, many of these dogs die before anyone sees them, so time is of the essence in their treatment. The longer the condition is present, the more breakdowns of body systems occur and irreversible damage to the stomach itself. The gas-filled stomach presses so hard on the diaphragm that it greatly impairs the dog's ability to breathe.

Dreading the ordeal ahead, but reassuring Dan that he had done just the right thing, I told him I was on my way to the clinic. When I got there, it was clear that Dan had been accurate in his diagnosis. The patient was verging on a moribund condition. His breathing was rapid and shallow, his tongue was a pale gray, and his stomach had dilated like the Hindenburg. I quickly started running through the procedures we would have to follow and found Dan to be an excellent assistant. We had the dog on intravenous fluids, sedated, and prepared for surgery in record time. I reviewed with him what I would be doing and what his responsibilities were. In breaks during the conversation, he still kept murmuring his apologies for having bothered me. I explained that no veterinarian, no matter how experienced, would attempt to treat a gastric torsion alone.

Always wanting to reinforce the new associate's standing as a full-fledged veterinarian, I told Dan that I would be the main surgeon and he would be my assistant and that perhaps the next case he would be the surgeon. This was placing the bar a little high, I thought, but wanted this to be a positive experience for my assistant.

As I opened the abdomen, my heart sank. The stomach wall was black, indicating death of the tissue. It looked as though we were probably too late. If the stomach wall dies, the animal goes through a downward spiral and is essentially irretrievable. I started cushioning Dan for the likely outcome of this case. I explained the prognosis and that most likely we would lose our patient regardless of our efforts. I knew he would somehow feel guilty, although there was no need to; he had done a fine job.

The surgery continued but my hopes did not rise. It is usually a heroic task to sort out the twist of the hideously bloated organ and get it returned to its original location. Often, as in this case, the spleen is also involved and too damaged to function. It is removed in these instances, making the surgery longer and more arduous. I explained everything as I went, but Dan didn't have much to say in response. I knew he was stressed, but he was doing a good job of following all my instructions. The color of the stomach never improved even after the twist was resolved and massive fluid and shock medication administered.

Several hours had passed. I had Dan pass a tube from the dog's mouth into its stomach to prevent the gas from building up any more. I continued to compliment him as he completed each task. I chatted with him and warned him that these difficult cases, ironically, often die just as the skin incision is closed. Dan continued to look miserable despite any reassurances I provided. Over and over, I repeated the litany that if the patient died, it was not because we hadn't done our best. Survival rates are low with this condition.

I was particularly concerned that the rest of the dog's bowel showed no sign of activity. The intestine was full of air but did not contract at all. After gastrointestinal surgery, it is always encouraging for the surgeon to see waves of contraction start to move through the exposed bowel as we are closing the incision. Nothing even suggestive of a contraction was occurring in this case.

Finally, I was done, and despite my gloomy predictions, the patient was still alive. His heartbeat sounded strong and the color of his mucus membranes had improved somewhat. I still refused to allow our hopes to rise. We started cleaning up the surgery room while we left the patient breathing oxygen to improve its tissue saturation. All the time, I was keeping up a fairly one-sided conversation. My poor new associate was apparently in the depths of depression about this operation. I was just glad we had gotten this far and felt it would be a good learning experience for him on many levels.

I asked Dan to monitor the patient, and I began taking armloads of instruments, drapes, and other equipment from the surgery room into the treatment area where I put them in cleaning solution to soak. This made the staff's work easier in the morning when they arrived.

I returned to the surgery room for more items. As I entered, I got the distinct smell of foul intestinal gas. I was elated. I said, "Dan! Do you smell that smell? That's great! That means that the dog's bowel is beginning to contract. He just might make it."

Dan did not share my enthusiasm. Maybe he was just too tired to respond. I grabbed another armload and headed back to the treatment room. I was allowing myself to believe now, and despite the late hour, my step was as bouncy as the dog's stomach had been earlier this evening. I began to whistle a little tune.

On my return, there was a veritable blue cloud hanging over the surgery room. I was determined that Dan should share my excitement and realize the implication of this noxious smell.

"Dan! That's perfume to a gut surgeon's nose. That's the sweetest smell you can smell after doing bowel surgery."

He cast his eyes down and stared at his feet in silence.

Now I was flummoxed. What else could I say? Then Dan spoke.

"I'm sorry Dr. Stronk. That's me you smell."

Addendum: our patient survived, but Dr. Dan's self-esteem did not.

CHAPTER 20
Whisper's Little Secret

Whisper was coming. Fire up the X-ray machine, hang a bag of intravenous fluids, check the surgical supplies. We're in for a long ride.

On Friday afternoon, the pace at the clinic takes a definite turn. As in most every other office, the staff looks forward to the weekend. We fervently hope that no challenging case will present itself when we have begun to put our minds on cruise control. The unfortunate exception is the doctor who will be working that particular weekend. That poor soul is trying to avoid the discussions about weekend plans and frivolous entertainment. They will be on emergency duty all weekend and putting in a full workday of appointments on Saturday. Since there is only one doctor on duty, the appearance of any daytime emergencies or the need to deal with extremely ill animals can really complicate the situation. And so, we all hope for what we call "a quiet weekend" that begins Friday afternoon and ends at 8:00 AM Monday.

On this particular Friday, the schedule was light and our professional demands limited. We were all starting to focus on the good times planned for the next two days. At mid-afternoon, several of us had gathered in the break room when the receptionist came in to discuss a caller she had on the phone. There was no need to explain once she said, "It's Whisper's owner."

Everyone knew what that meant. Whisper was a legend in the clinic—sixty-five muscular pounds of male boxer that viewed any item as a culinary challenge. The list of objects we had removed from Whisper's gut either surgically or medically included several TV remotes, a transistor radio, panty hose, socks, earrings, coins, rocks, and wire. His fetish leaned more toward plastics, and none of the material he ingested appeared even remotely related to a food item. He just seemed to enjoy the challenge of stuffing items into his big wide jaws and swallowing. The owners now had veritable veterinary certification in recognizing the symptoms associated with the gastrointestinal complaints that indicated foreign body ingestion and/or blockage. They rarely witnessed the crime but had come to know the first signs and brought him in immediately.

It was Dr. Steve's weekend on duty, so he would see the case. He had not been with our practice very long but had come to us with several years of experience. What he lacked was our knowledge of the patient's colorful history. This patient would undoubtedly involve prolonged care, possibly even surgery. I assured him that the initial part would be easy. The diagnosis would only be a matter of finding out *what* not *if* he had ingested.

Dr. Steve did not look excited by the prospect even though we handed him his diagnosis. He was experienced enough to know he was seeing his weekend already degenerating before his eyes. I told him to do his usual exam, and then regardless of his findings, take Whisper to X-ray and try to visualize what the current alien matter was.

X-rays can be wonderfully helpful, but they are not the complete answer in these cases. The denser the foreign matter is, such as a stone or nail, the better it will show up. If the object is softer but has a distinct shape such as a tennis ball, we can often make that out as well.

With objects that are less dense, it becomes a matter of conjecture. By looking at the gas pattern or placement of various parts of the bowel, we can get an indication that there is probably something there but cannot be entirely sure from an X-ray. This is the case with cloth and paper items.

Dr. Steve left our happy group to meet his patient. As he exited, we cheerfully called out, "Don't forget the X-ray!" One would think we were sending him out for grocery items.

Eventually, the door to the break room opened and a fresh X-ray brandished in the air. Dr. Steve shook his head and said that although the dog did indeed have all the symptoms of having a gastrointestinal foreign body, all that showed up was one paper clip in his stomach. He was very doubtful that one little paper clip could cause the magnitude of symptoms he was seeing, classic for a foreign body. The dog was not eating, hadn't passed stool in more than a day, would drink water and then vomit it back up, and walked with a slight arch to his back as though his abdomen was uncomfortable. This was the Whisper we all knew and dreaded to see.

Although I agreed with Dr. Steve, I still thought it was best to get the paper clip out of Whisper's stomach before it passed into his intestines. When an object is small and fairly smooth, the easiest mode of elimination is to induce vomiting. For this purpose, we usually use apomorphine. This is a drug related to morphine, but its effects are very different. Whereas morphine is a blessing in the face of pain, apomorphine is the evil side of our pharmacopeia—it induces severe, stomach-emptying retching almost immediately when administered. The mode of administration is also quite interesting. The medication comes in tiny pellets. One of these pellets, not much bigger than a mustard seed, is placed inside the pouch of the lower eyelid of the patient. As the tears start to soften it, it is absorbed into the system. The good part is that as soon as it has done its work, we flush the eye out with sterile saline and the effects of the drug stop. This is often grand theater, and those of us not otherwise occupied, trooped back to the treatment room to watch the show. I had to wonder if Whisper, so used to this routine, might not start feeling nauseous just watching us go to the safe where we keep the apomorphine.

Dr. Steve retrieved the bottle of tiny pellets, got his flush ready, and watched us take up our positions on stools and countertops. The Romans arranged themselves in the arena ready to witness the spectacle. Possibly, out of respect for the dog, or perhaps considering clean-up matters, Dr. Steve decided to administer the dose in the kennel area. Feeling a bit cheated, we sat and continued to chat among ourselves. Time passed and eventually Dr. Steve reappeared with Whisper on a leash. He placed him in a large cage in the treatment area. We were all waiting expectantly. Well? Was the paper clip out?

He couldn't be sure. Whisper had produced a lot of vomit and the paper clip was small. There would have to be a thorough investigation. He collected some gloves and a handful of tongue depressors and went to perform the disgusting task of dissecting the mess. To his credit, he could have passed this job to an unfortunate technician, but he chose to do it himself.

The minute Dr. Steve disappeared behind the kennel door, the treatment area resounded to an unearthly retching noise. Actually, it sounded like "Harf!" All eyes turned to Whisper expecting an alien creature to burst forth from his chest. He braced his legs, shook his head with slobber flying everywhere, opened his big jaws to their maximum stretch, gave one heave, and produced a foul, slimy mass from the depths of his stomach. If I had not witnessed it myself, I would never have believed what was encased within the stomach of that dog. I sprang up and released Whisper from the confines of his cage, anxious to examine the object. To my surprise, it was an entire carpet sample, the squares found on display at stores. And neatly snagged in the middle of the sample was one paper clip. The dog had swallowed the carpet whole. The edges weren't even frayed.

Immediately, a technician jumped up and offered to give Dr. Steve the good news and abort the disgusting task he had begun. I thought about it a moment and then said, "Let's just leave him alone. I don't want to discourage him from being thorough." There were some giggles among us evil, soon-to-be-enjoying-our weekend people.

Moments later, Dr. Steve appeared looking crestfallen. He was shaking his head and contemplating the need for surgical intervention on Whisper and a tedious start to his work weekend.

"Did you find it?" I asked.

He shook his head and said that he guessed that the clip might now be down in the dog's intestines, a worse location for surgical intervention.

I asked if he wanted the good news or the bad news first. He looked up, confused, and said he'd like the bad news first. I told him that he had just wasted the last fifteen minutes. He looked even more confused.

"And here's the good news," I said and held up the carpet sample.

I thought he would faint from relief or shock. I trusted my astute fellow workers to avoid mentioning at what exact moment we had become privy to this bit of information. Some things are best left unspoken.

CHAPTER 21
A Cat's Tale

The distraught woman burst through the front door of the clinic. She was carrying her cat wrapped in a towel and clutching it to her chest. The receptionist rushed in to get me. We finally extracted the story: a vacuum cleaner had sucked up the cat's tail.

I gently took the cat, had the woman sit down in the waiting room, and brought the feline into the treatment room for evaluation.

The plump, orange tabby was serene and seemingly unfazed by what had transpired. I removed the towel expecting blood and lacerations. The towel was dry and the cat still acted as though nothing had happened. Then I looked at the end of the tail and was shocked to see that the last few inches were just dry, white bone. There was no trace of blood or skin.

In the accident, it appeared that the blood vessels had been stretched, retracted, and sealed immediately. I assumed the nerves had been cut so quickly that the cat was not even in any pain. It was fairly grotesque, but I could see why the owner was so upset and guilt-stricken. The cat had a normal furry tail except for several inches of skeleton protruding from the end of it.

I made the cat comfortable and went out to discuss the treatment with the owner. I assured her the cat was comfortable, but that I would have to amputate the exposed portion of the tail. This was an uncomplicated procedure and in a week or two, the cat would heal. I tried to assuage her guilty feelings.

I also tried to extract from her the manufacturer of her vacuum cleaner. You see, I never seemed to find a vacuum cleaner that could adequately clean the floor at home and stay in some semblance of running order. Over the years, I went through several models, hoping to find a sturdy workhorse that would satisfy me.

After buying one particular model that sported a well-known brand, I was particularly disappointed. One lackluster performance followed another, always wasting my limited time and energy. Finally, it coughed, buzzed, and passed out. I returned the vacuum cleaner to the store where I had purchased it. The technician admitted it as though to a hospital, and told me he would contact me when he finished troubleshooting the problem. I was on the verge of shooting it myself.

Several days passed, and I received a call informing me that the vacuum was now ready to go home. When I arrived, the technician gave me a particularly disapproving look. He asked if we had anyone in the house with long hair. We had three females in the house so there was no denying that fact; we had plenty of hair. He then informed me that my problem was from hair lodged in the vacuum. He told me I should always go through the house before vacuuming and pick up all the hair first.

I had never heard of such a ridiculous thing before. If I was going to go through all of that, why have a vacuum cleaner at all? I took the hateful thing home. The next time I vacuumed the house, I was anxious to see how the repair work had affected the machine's capabilities. The minute I started it up, the power went out on our side of town for the remainder of the afternoon. And so my search went for several years.

Consequently, I just had to know what kind of vacuum cleaner had enough power to suck the tail off a cat. A small, evil voice in my head demanded my attention as I tried to soothe the distraught cat owner. I tried to ignore the voice, but it would not be denied. I wrestled with the need to be professional, but the voice would not be quiet. I considered the woman's shattered emotional state but the voice was relentless. How could I miss this once in a lifetime opportunity?

I couched my inquiries around the accident as though the exact sequence of events was important knowledge to a surgeon faced with this amputation. As it turned out, the vacuum had a carpet beater bar, and once caught in the suction, the tail was grabbed by the bar.

I had almost achieved my goal; the vacuum prize was before me. I pondered a moment and then casually asked, "What make of vacuum would that be? I mean, what horsepower do you think it has?"

Of course, the poor woman couldn't remember, but the little voice had demanded that I at least try.

Years passed, and we received the inevitable request from a vacuum sales representative to come to our house to demonstrate his marvelous machine. We were still in the throes of vacuum hell, and I told him that he could come to the house, as he was offering a free cleaning, making it an attractive offer for me.

The sales representative was a pleasant and hardworking man. It was a hot, humid summer evening, and he went through many dirt-defying feats with our rug, furniture, and floors. By the time he was finished, there was sweat dripping from his forehead. He was truly determined.

While he was there, my husband decided to share the amazing story of "The Vacuum That Could Suck the Tail off a Cat." He laughed appreciatively. I could imagine this one going the rounds over a few drinks at the next vacuum sales representative's convention he attended.

We received the sales pitch and he waited expectantly for our response. We are not impulse buyers, and although he had put on a good show and we were both impressed, there was no way that we would make such a purchase without spending some time thinking about it

The representative persisted. He wanted us to buy the machine, and he wanted the sale closed *tonight.* He pulled a few more tricks out of his bag to demonstrate the remarkable capabilities of this machine. It appeared awesome among vacuums but we wouldn't budge.

Finally, he asked, "What would I have to do tonight to convince you to buy the machine right now?"

There was a long pause. We were tired and cranky. John looked over at me, sighed, and said purposefully, "Okay, honey, go get the cat."

The sales representative grabbed his equipment and fled, looking slightly terrified. We did buy the vacuum from him later in the week.

CHAPTER 22
The Sole Evidence

"There's blood everywhere. It looks like a slaughterhouse." That was all I needed to hear. There was no point in any further questioning. I instructed the caller to put the cat in a carrier and head for my clinic where I would meet him in twenty minutes. Although I had barely had time to take my coat off, I shrugged it back on. As I exited my cozy house, the full moon shone down on me and the irony was not lost. Every veterinarian knows that being on emergency duty on the night of a full moon means there will be little rest for the weary.

The elderly man who had called was housesitting for one of my clients. He had sounded anxious and a bit confused. Upon his arrival at my client's home that evening to feed the cat, he had found blood in the kitchen. He had described more than a few drips of blood. His voice had shaken as he assured me that it was "a *lot* of blood." Although confined to the house since the departure of my client, the caller was sure that the cat had some kind of accident. He had been unable to discover the source of the cat's bleeding. I asked if there was blood on its fur, and he said that there was not.

As I drove, I mentally reviewed any cause of significant blood loss in a house cat that would leave no traces on the fur. I wasn't getting very far with my options when I reached the clinic. The caller and the cat hadn't arrived yet, so I quickly retrieved the cat's record from our files and looked it over trying to discern if the cat had any history of bleeding problems. This record was absolutely the most boring piece of literature we had in our files. The cat had walked the straight and narrow path all of its life. It was vaccinated on time and never had any type of accident or illness that brought him to our attention. The annual examination showed every body system to be within normal limits. No clues here.

When I saw headlights approaching, I unlocked the front door and stood behind the reception desk holding the cat's record. As soon as the older fellow opened the front door, I greeted him from behind the counter, turned, and led him into the examination room where I took up my usual post behind the exam table. He placed the carrier on the table and I gently removed the cat. I glanced into the carrier but saw no trace of blood. Whatever the problem was, it appeared the bleeding had stopped, at least temporarily.

My patient looked quite surprised but definitely alert and responsive. I quickly checked his gum color, concerned that he had lost a significant amount of blood. To my relief, his gums and tongue were a vibrant healthy pink. There was no evidence of blood tinge in his saliva or down his throat. I quickly ticked off my problem list. I peered into each ear. A blow to the head can cause hemorrhage from the ear canal. Both ears were a lovely pale shell pink. I ran my hands over the cat's body. No moisture, swellings, or painful areas found. The cat did not object to anything I did. In fact, I would swear that it looked a little confused.

I proceeded to palpate his abdomen, starting out very gingerly, and then seeing that he was unperturbed, I made my manipulations more thorough. Again, there were no complaints or resistance to my ministrations. I gave particular care to palpating the bladder, unwilling to give up my theory that bloody urine was what the man had actually seen. The bladder was moderately full and definitely not painful. If the cat had a urinary tract infection severe enough to lose that much blood, his bladder should have been exquisitely painful. I was running out of possibilities. I watched the man's look of concern as I went through my examination. He kept repeating that there had been a lot of blood as if he thought I did not believe him. I kept up a running commentary explaining what I was doing and reassuring him as I ruled out various possibilities. The only thing left to do was to take the cat's temperature. Besides garnering the actual body temperature, by examining the thermometer after I removed it, I would be able to tell if the cat had any blood in his stool by checking what clung to the instrument.

I had the thermometer in place and waited the mandatory time for it to register when I realized that I had heard a sporadic, soft, odd noise. It was a moist noise, kind of a "squish." We had stopped talking while the thermometer was in place as if unnecessary chatter would interfere with its function. (Clients will invariably carry on one-sided conversations as I attempt to auscultate the heart and lungs, but conversation grinds to a halt when I wield the old fever stick.)

I was definitely aware of the sound. I concentrated and realized it did not seem to be coming from my patient. As I pondered this, my eyes wandered up and away from the table and strayed out the exam room door to the waiting room. Something was not right. I focused on the floor out there and to my shock, saw a trail of bloody footprints leading from the front door to the exam room. It then became clear that the squishing noises coincided with the cat's caregiver shifting his weight back and forth. With a little sick feeling in the pit of my stomach, I slowly bent over and peeked under the exam table.

The footprints led right up to the man and ended in a pool of blood around his right sneaker. As he again shifted his weight, I heard the squish and saw the pool enlarge a tiny bit. I was working on the wrong patient!

"Sir, the cat is not bleeding, *you are!*"

He was polite but quickly denied it could be him. I had to insist that he look at his own foot. He appeared mildly perplexed by his situation but was clearly relieved that the cat he was caring for was all right.

I scooped the cat into the carrier, told him that I would hold the cat for the night, and that he needed to get to a doctor. He smiled and informed me that he would have his son take him in the morning.

Clearly, he was not as impressed with the degree of blood loss as I was. I insisted he go to the local emergency room immediately. I asked if he had injured himself in any way. He was sure that he had not and was in no pain. It took a lot of convincing to get him to agree to see a physician immediately. I was thinking that I should remove his shoe and dress whatever wound he might have but reconsidered. The sneaker may have been acting like a pressure bandage, and I couldn't take a chance that the hemorrhage would escalate.

I called the local emergency room and gave them warning of what I was sending their way. I did not trust my elderly friend to convey the story as it had unfolded. I followed up with the emergency room later. The poor fellow had a minor wound but was on blood thinners for a heart condition and so his blood was not clotting properly. The doctor thanked me for getting him to their attention.

With the caregiver tended to, I placed the cat in a kennel with water and a litter pan, put a cage card with his identification on the door, and prepared to leave. Many people feel that cats lack facial expression but I disagree. The look I got from this cat spoke volumes. If it could speak, I imagine this is what had been going through his mind:

Life is good. Very good. The humans I allow to share my abode have been gone for several days. I do not need to be distracted by their comings and goings. No need to act interested in their feeble attempts to play with me. More importantly, I can spread out and truly enjoy my realm without having to hear, "No! Bad kitty!"

My days are filled with leisure. I hop up on the kitchen counter, which is normally taboo. From here, I can watch the bird feeder and daydream about imagined kills. I explore the entire countertop but find nothing of interest. I occasionally sit for a session of grooming, letting my shed fur settle gently on the Formica. Later, I will give myself a refreshing workout on the human's favorite chair. I can see why they like it so much. It is an excellent surface to give purchase to my saber-like claws. I notice the corner that faces the living room is starting to show a nice worn fuzziness due to my ministrations.

In their absence, I have found a new taste delight. A hanging spider plant is usually well beyond my reach. They have left it in the bathroom sink, obviously intending it for me. I snack on the leaves and have started digging in the pot. It shows great promise as an alternative bathroom should the Visitor forget to keep my litter pan scrupulously clean. The smaller plants that dangle from the main foliage amuse me. I can visualize them as small birds before I snare them out of the air and consume them.

I spend the afternoon napping on the humans' bed. Not at the foot of the bed where they insist I sleep when they are in residence, but couched in the lovely down pillows at the head, much more in keeping with my station in life.

I look ahead to the evening, when the Visitor will arrive. His face is vaguely familiar to me but of little consequence in my life. He refills my food and water dish, cleans and refreshes my bathroom facilities. I occasionally condescend to allow him to stroke my head. It seems to make him happy. Usually, I retreat under the kitchen table and glare at him. I cannot allow him to feel appreciated and assume airs in my home.

On this particular evening; however, as soon as the Visitor entered the kitchen, I sensed something was different. There was a distinct pungent odor. Then I saw it! He left blood on the kitchen floor everywhere he walked. I became dizzy with expectation. Could it be that this human realized the lack of flavor or enticement in the dry kibble I am served day after day? Had he just returned from a successful hunt bearing tidbits? My mind danced with images of a fat mole, or dare I hope, a house sparrow? He continued to walk about, speaking in the language that humans use.

I followed his every move, waiting for the unveiling of my culinary delight. Perhaps it was still alive and would have some play value. He went to the box that humans converse with on the wall and continued to stall. I was beside myself with excitement. After leaving the talk box, he made a brief trip down into the underworld below the living quarters. I do not go there; it's another forbidden activity. When he came back into the kitchen, I was too agitated to notice what he had brought. Having abandoned caution, I allowed him to scoop me up in his arms. To my horror, I soon realized what he had fetched. It was the dreaded Transport Cubicle.

The door yawned open and before I could mount a decent objection, he stuffed me into its gaping maw.

The Transport Cubicle is a place of horror to all cats. Once inside, anything can happen. I suspect it is involved with time travel. Anytime I enter, I exit in another world and I have lost any sense of how long I have been gone. And so it is this time, only worse. I had never done time travel at night. There were the usual slamming noises, deep roars, and grumbling sounds. Lights flashed erratically, and I was thrown from side to side as I was whisked through the universe. I howled mournfully, hardly able to believe I had allowed myself to be duped in this way.

Suddenly the portal opened and I was in a new galaxy. There was light and strange chemical odors. I could hear the distant howl and bark of wild animals. A female human who is somewhat familiar, extracted me from the cubicle. It suddenly occurred to me what had happened. Somehow, the humans knew I had broken all their rules. My outlaw life was no longer a secret. I was going to be placed on trial and judged for my deeds. They would get nothing out of me. I went into a deep meditative trance facilitated by activating the Purr Box.

My inquisitor spoke softly, but I could tell she could be tough if necessary. She opened my mouth and peered inside. Was she looking for bits of spider plant between my teeth? I tried to remember the last time I had consumed any, hoping all traces were washed away. She stared deeply into my eyes. I didn't flinch. I even refused to focus on her face. I was a rock. She slid her hands over my body. I refused to cringe or show fear. She grew bolder, probing more deeply. I showed her the tough feline that I am. It was nothing to me.

Next, there was a minute examination of my pads and claws. Certainly, she was looking for shreds of cloth from the favored chair. It's too late. I could do nothing about that now. I considered lashing out and giving her a taste of my paws of steel but decided to wait and resort to violence only when the time was obviously right.

She placed an instrument in her ears and attached it to me with a long black tube. She was extricating vital information from me against my will. I made my mind a blank to foil her attempts. I was inscrutable.

The inquisition finally seemed to be winding down. I entertained the thought that I had won. The humans spoke back and forth in tongues. Then the unthinkable happened. The female human turned, grasped a glass rod, shook it in the air, and lifted my tail. I cannot record the despicable deed that followed, but I will say that I remained strong and did not give in.

Suddenly everything changed. I was jammed back into the Transport Cubicle. There was a great deal of excited noise back and forth between the humans. Eventually the Visitor was ushered out. I was left with my torturer, and I dared not imagine what would happen next. Even without my cooperation, she had obviously divined my secret life of crime and reckless pleasure.

She carried me back into the bowels of the building, ever closer to the wild beasts shrieking for attention. This must be the famous Gulag that cats speak of when they gather in dark alleyways. I was thrust into a larger cubicle with nothing but a bowl of water. (This was not my usual well water either, I detected the odor of chlorine. Perhaps I will be poisoned!) There was a public bathroom in one corner. Although it seemed clean enough, there was absolutely no privacy. I was distraught. The remains of my last spider plant meal felt like a giant hairball in my stomach.

She smiled at me and stroked my chin. What blatant deceit! The lights were turned out and I was alone. I found solace. Craftily, I slithered under the papers covering the floor of the cubicle. Hidden from human eyes, I no longer existed. I activated the Purr Box and lulled myself to sleep.

I made a mental note that if I were returned to my abode, I would avoid the favored human chair for scratching purposes. I would promptly lose my newfound taste for houseplants. As soon as the humans return, I would wind myself around their legs in a joyous show of adoration. I only hoped it would be enough to override their reaction to all my fur on their pillows.

CHAPTER 23
Here and Then Gone

No farmer had ever fainted on me. I had one who casually turned away as I was removing a particularly foul smelling retained placenta from his cow. He vomited in the gutter, carefully wiped his mouth with a handkerchief, and continued his conversation with me. I had never had to deal with an owner that "checked out." All this would change when I moved into a mixed practice situation my second year out of veterinary school, and I had to learn to deal with each circumstance in a novel way.

Not prepared for the mind-set of small animal clientele, I had no idea of the power of the spoken word. I had not even imagined the high anxiety that I could produce wielding nothing but a telephone receiver.

An ailing poodle with a list of written complaints was dropped off at the clinic where I worked. I spent considerable time examining my patient and running pertinent laboratory exams. I was rather excited to find that the dog was suffering from an autoimmune disorder that caused destruction of blood platelets prematurely and at an alarming rate. This predisposed the dog to bleed abnormally. We had learned about this case in a textbook at school, and I was quite proud of myself for having made the diagnosis. It was not a common problem, and I felt exhilarated at having made this diagnosis for the first time in my career. I was ready with a plan for treatment and felt prepared to discuss with the owner at length the long-term implications of the disease.

Pumped up with self-importance, I dialed the pet owner's number. As soon as she answered, I identified myself and launched into an explanation of my examination, the results of the laboratory work, my projected treatment plan, and the prognosis, or expected outcome. At some point in my verbal exuberance, I began to think that the owner seemed unusually quiet and didn't have many questions for me. Unfazed, I continued at breakneck speed, unleashing all the pent up knowledge that I had acquired in four grueling years of graduate study.

When I was forced to pause for breath, I waited for a response. At that point, I heard an awful crash on the telephone line followed by silence.

I was at a loss to explain what might be happening. I called out the owner's name but received no response. I repeated this several times, getting louder and louder, when it suddenly occurred to me that the person at the other end of the telephone must not be conscious. What to do?

I was frantic. I had visions of lawsuits dancing in my mind. I imagined my employer terminating me for whatever gross malpractice I had just committed. I was clueless as to what I had done wrong, but I knew that it must have been very bad.

I continued to hold the phone and called the owner's name repeatedly. I entertained the thought of calling an ambulance but thought I'd be considered a lunatic if I did. What would I be reporting? A dead phone line?

Finally, a new tone came on the telephone line, another female voice. She demanded to know who I was and what I had just told the original party. Numb, I began listing the things I had covered concerning the poodle. I was cut off quickly, and the new party insisted on knowing if I had delivered bad news. I had to stop and think.

Finally, I said, "Well, not really. I think the dog will be all right before too long. It's a treatable condition."

She informed me that my client had fainted and was unconscious on the floor. Then she hung up, and left me to consider my sins.

Time dragged and I was in agony. Every possible terrible scenario paraded before my mind's eye. Had I killed this poor woman with my heartless diatribe? Was she in an ambulance or in some intensive care unit? I dared not call the number again, so I waited, and waited, and waited.

In retrospect, I realize that my only mistake was my lamentable enthusiasm for my topic. Swept up in the excitement of a novel diagnosis, I hadn't spent much time on the human element of the scene. Having no previous history with the client, I had not attempted to forge a human connection and had just charged forward with too much information, too technical, too fast. Unfortunately, because of my youth and inexperience, I was not aware of this, and so I sat at the clinic stewing over the possibility that I had telepathically murdered a client.

Eventually I received a call, and thankfully, it was the client herself on the line. I anxiously inquired about her health and well-being. She sounded fine. I apologized for any distress that I had caused her. Anxious to ensure that I would never repeat this scene, I asked what I had done or said that had alarmed her to such an extent that she had fainted.

"Well, you just kept talking about blood," she replied.

Good to know.

***

Experience with dog training can be an unexpected bonus in the veterinary clinic. This is especially true when cross training occurs and humans respond as a dog might.

Years later, my husband and I owned a small animal practice in Vermont. He was the business manager and worked out of an office behind the reception area. At the time, I was in an advanced stage of pregnancy.

We had just opened for business one morning when an upset local farmer came rushing in the front door carrying his dog. His instantly recognizable last name was that of a family who had significant economic impact on our country. And yes, he was a direct descendant of that line of the family. He had chosen farming for its simple, hardworking lifestyle. Unfortunately, he had backed up his tractor that morning not knowing his dog was behind it and the machine had struck the animal.

I quickly ushered him into an examination room and had him place the dog on the table. I began evaluating the dog, talking as I did so, and letting him know all my findings. The farmer just kept mumbling and repeating how awful he felt for having injured his own dog. I was as reassuring as possible. It was clear the dog could not use one of its front legs and that the cause was a bone fracture.

I concluded my examination and began to tell him that I would need to keep the dog for X-rays and observation. When I looked up from the dog, I saw the man's usual, healthy ruddy face was a sick shade of green. His eyes were just beginning to roll back, and I immediately knew he was a fraction of a second from hitting the floor.

There is no explanation for the mental gymnastics that go on in such a situation. I made the decision that keeping his head from splitting open on the floor or the exam table took precedence over the welfare of his dog. I should also mention that this fellow was a big, big, strapping man. I dived from behind the exam table to intercept him as he went down like a felled oak tree. We both ended up on the floor, his torso laid out across my legs, pinning me with my very pregnant belly to the floor. I had managed to cradle his head in the fall, and I was pleased that it had not touched the floor.

The dog, frightened by the sudden flurry of activity, leaped from the exam table and flew out the door, shrieking as its broken leg tried to support its weight in the jump. The canine disappeared down the hall, caterwauling all the way. Chaos reigned and I was completely immobilized by my insensate load.

I needed someone strong to move this fellow, so I began yelling for my husband, John. I didn't know it then, but John was on the phone and could clearly hear the shrieking dog. Imagining that I just needed help in examining an uncooperative patient, he figured any of the technicians would come to my assistance and continued with his phone call.

Minutes passed and my new human patient was beginning to show signs of life. As he slowly regained his wits, he was shocked to find himself on the floor in my lap, and even more shocked to hear his dog shrieking. I assured him the dog would be just fine, though it continued yelping down the hall. I had no idea what was happening to the dog.

Embarrassed, he attempted to lunge to his feet. Knowing he was not ready to stand and fearing another fall, I asked him to wait a few moments. I slid out from under him and as I got to my feet, he again lurched upward trying to stand.

I resorted to my best dog trainer routine. I looked at him sternly, pointed one finger, and announced with great authority, "Sit! Stay!"

Miraculously, this worked quite well. He leaned against a wall and seemed content to wait for a bit. I told him I would get him a glass of water and after that, he could try getting up. Eventually, he regained his composure and was able to rise without difficulty. He was ashamed of what had happened although it was completely understandable. In a state of extreme anxiety and rushing in from the cold outdoors to a warm room, he had suddenly been overcome. I reassured him not to be concerned. Finally, he got to the crux of the problem.

"Please, don't tell my wife," he implored of me.

I assured him that it was our little secret.

***

Sometimes we are forced to walk awhile in another's shoes. Months after my sumo match with the farmer, John found himself in an equally embarrassing situation. One of our clients, the famous Satellite Jack, had arranged to have a house call for his kennel of Chow Chow dogs. They needed various vaccinations and tests, and since they did not travel well, he wanted them all cared for at the same time at his kennel.

My associate, Dr. Bob, agreed to go out and take care of them while John assisted. I was thrilled with this arrangement, because it left me completely out of the picture. Several of the dogs had shown themselves to be untrustworthy, which is a veterinary euphemism for the fact that given any chance, they would bite. One big male in particular was a terror to handle. My colleague prided himself in being able to handle the brute, and the two fellows left one cold early spring day to do their manly deed.

They were gone for hours, quite a bit longer than we had anticipated. When they finally returned, it was immediately clear that not all had gone as they had hoped. Dr. Bob was wearing a wet undershirt and sporting bandages wrapped all over one hand and wrist. He looked pale and walked past me with his head hanging.

John took me aside and filled me in on what happened. The owner would bring one of the dogs out to the table in the kennel and John would restrain it while Dr. Bob performed the exam and other ministrations. Most of the dogs were behaving well and the procedure was going smoothly. Then they got to the infamous male, Satan's Spawn of dogdom.

Dr. Bob had made his first advance to the dog, talked to him, and attempted to pet him. Then before anyone could do anything to restrain the dog, the Chow bit Dr. Bob's hand and wrist several times leaving many deep puncture wounds. The owner, understandably upset and apologetic, pulled the dog off the doctor. Dr. Bob just stared at his wounds, and then suggested they go to the vehicle and get some bandages. They went outside and John started to prepare the bandage materials.

"I don't feel very well," Dr. Bob had said. He became flush and began to sweat despite the cold temperature outside. He stripped off his jacket and then his shirt and stood in the freezing weather in only an undershirt. Then the familiar cascade of symptoms began with the greening of the face, shaking, and certain collapse. Knowing this was a direct reaction to the dog bite, John helped him lie down.

Looking down at our prostrate, very large associate unceremoniously lying flat on his back in a partially unclad state, John began to think things couldn't get much worse. But, of course, they did. Big, fluffy, light flakes of classic Vermont snow began to lazily drift down and settle on Dr. Bob's seemingly lifeless body. Only time was going to get Dr. Bob back on his feet, so John waited it out, hoping he wouldn't become hypothermic. At the same time, he wondered what Satellite Jack's take on this scene would be if he came looking for them.

To his credit, Dr. Bob eventually came to, allowed John to wrap the wounds, and he even managed to finish the work he had to do. Veterinarians tend to be made of pretty stern stuff.

***

"Are you kidding? I *love* blood and guts!" The bravado of my middle school observer was almost overwhelming. Unfortunately, we can never tell in advance who may reveal themselves as faint of heart.

219

It would be so convenient to issue them a helmet and kneepads as they entered the clinic but they always tend to sneak up on me.

I am often asked to allow schoolchildren to come into the clinic to observe or job shadow. This can be fun if the tempo of activity is relaxed, but can be stressful if emergencies crop up while we are shepherding a youngster. The middle school in my town had an active job-shadowing program. I was asked to allow a young woman named Ali to spend a morning observing at the clinic. I was happy to comply; however, we had some difficulty working out a mutually agreeable date. I finally discussed possible dates with the young woman herself on the telephone. It seemed that the only day she had a light class schedule happened to be my surgery day. I explained that she would be under my direct supervision. On that morning, I wouldn't be seeing office appointments but would be doing a series of surgical procedures. She was thrilled. I explained that she would have to follow instructions very carefully. There would be some blood involved, although I planned to have very limited procedures that were not likely to be bloody.

She was all for the opportunity and said that she actually preferred to see surgery. Since she lived in the same town I did, I said I'd provide transportation for her that morning. The details were finalized, and the day for her grand adventure arrived.

I picked Ali up at her house on the assigned morning. Ali was not a shy wallflower. On the drive to the clinic, she entertained me with her experiences with animals and all the amazing medical ministrations she had already seen with various species. This young woman was a real talker. When we arrived at the clinic, I gave her a brief tour and introduced her all around. I did a few treatments; she was full of questions and observations. Mainly, she wanted to know when we were going to get down to it and get into surgery.

The first surgery was a kitten from the local humane society to be spayed. This is probably the most bloodless surgery we do on a routine basis. The kittens weigh only three or four pounds and the uterus is not much larger around than a strand of knitting yarn. The ovaries look like pale peas.

I told Ali that she had to stand in an assigned spot, and no matter what, she could not move closer to the surgery table or touch me. She could not touch anything on the table or surgery tray either. She was impatient to get the proceedings going and assured me she understood the rules. I made sure again that she felt she would be able to handle being in a surgery room.

After performing my surgical scrub and donning sterile gloves, I opened my surgery pack and carefully placed a sterile drape over the kitten quietly sleeping under anesthesia on the table. Ali danced from foot to foot in her excitement to see the operation.

At this point, the kitten was completely covered by the drape and all we could hear was the quiet whoosh and beep from instruments monitoring the patient's vital signs. There is a small oval hole in the drape about one inch long positioned over the incision site. I made the skin incision, about a half-inch long, opened the abdomen, and quickly identified a horn of the uterus. There was not a drop of blood to be seen. I lifted the horn of the uterus so that Ali could see it and explained what I was holding. I commented on how marvelous it was that something that tiny would eventually be able to hold and incubate a litter of kittens in an adult cat. I gently moved the horn out a little more and the tiny ovary popped into sight. I again identified the structure for Ali and made sure she had a good view of it from her station. There was still not a drop of blood, and the kitten's heartbeat and respiration never varied.

Then the bells went off. For several minutes, I had not heard a single word from my rapt voyeur. I had been concentrating totally on my patient, of course, and had not been looking up at the student observer. As my stomach began to drop to my shoes, I looked up just in time to see Ali slithering down the wall of the surgery room. This time, I could do nothing. I had to respect my surgical patient, and it looked like the descent was going well for Ali. That is, until she bent her elbow as she went down.

Next to her was a cabinet holding drawers of extra surgical instruments. On top of the cabinet was a stainless steel cold tray used to hold various instruments in a cold disinfecting solution. As she slid past, her elbow hooked the tray and the entire contents, instruments, and green disinfectant solution slopped down the front of her and into her lap when she finally hit the floor. It was the most graceful and safest faint I have ever witnessed in my career, but it was really ruined by that cold tray.

All I could do was to yell, "Help!" and wait for reinforcements. Of course, my technician assumed there was some crisis with the surgery and came in on the run checking the patient's vital signs and anesthetic machine posthaste.

"No no no!" I said and nodded my head in the direction of the opposite wall. There was Ali, looking as if she had sat down to take a siesta against the wall with her legs splayed straight out in front of her, a lap full of surgery instruments, and the green disinfectant slowly soaking into her clothing. Ashley, my technician, rolled her eyes and went over to help remove the debris and reassure Ali as she began to regain consciousness.

Although we all repeatedly assured her that fainting was nothing to be ashamed of, Ali was clearly mortified. We gave her a set of scrub tops and pants so she could change out of her soaked clothing. I finished my surgeries in record time (while Ali was elsewhere in the building) and arranged to drive her home a little ahead of schedule.

The drive home was the exact opposite of our drive into the clinic. Ali sat stone-faced and silent. I tried to tell her about every incident that had ever happened to anyone I knew who had fainted, including a time I came very close to fainting my first week of veterinary school. I even complimented her on her style, so graceful and smooth. The poor child just would not talk. I think it would not have been so mortifying if she had not played the overblown braggart part initially. I made a mental note to myself: No more adolescents in the surgery room!

***

Ashley would be the last person to chide someone for fainting. She knows better than that. She knows that excitement, tension, and being overly anxious to perform well can contribute to the brain saying, "Enough for now, I'm shutting down."

Years ago, we had two students from a college veterinary technician program come to spend a few days observing at our practice. They were nice young women although quiet. They were able to follow all the work that went on in the laboratory, and we had them observe in the treatment room as we handled minor surgical cases.

During one of the observation days, I bent over to clean a cat's infected wound when I heard my assistant call out, "Watch out, the tall one's going!" I looked up and Ashley, the taller of the two young women, was on her way to the floor. Fortunately, her friend was able to help her as she crumpled. As expected, she was very embarrassed, although we assured her that she need not be.

Well, "the tall one" ended up applying for a position in our clinic upon graduation. I honestly forgot that she had even spent any time observing in our clinic. We hired Ashley ten years ago, and she has been my chief technician and right hand for many years. Although she rolled her eyes at Ali's plight, she would be the last person to jest about Ali's situation.

CHAPTER 24
Sickening Sweet

"Why can't dogs eat chocolate?" This continues to be a subject of fascination and amazement for most dog owners. Get over it. It's just a fact. When outside the clinic setting, such as at a social event, the minute the topic seems about to be introduced, I wish I had a sign that would pop up over my head that read, Please Don't Ask.

Everybody has a story about the time their dog ate chocolate and did or did not get ill, and everybody has to take their turn in telling their story. I however have been a participant in the epic, One Most Incredible Story of Canine Chocolate Consumption of All Time. Truth can be much stranger than fiction.

The holiday season brings a predictable wave of phone calls and sick patients. Human beings are not the only ones who overeat or ingest meals that are not on their usual menu. Christmas and Easter invariably generate a few calls about dogs that have gotten into the forbidden chocolate goodies and the darker the chocolate, the more severe the symptoms the dog experiences. In mild cases, the dog may just become agitated, uncomfortable, and tremble. In worst cases, they may have seizures and even die.

Just before Christmas one year, we received a phone call from a client whose dog had eaten a box of dark chocolate bars. When they realized what had happened, they called immediately, fully aware of the potential consequences. The reason they were so well educated was that two years before, just prior to Christmas, this dog had eaten a bag of chocolate chip cookies. Normally, this would not contain enough chocolate to cause toxic symptoms, and the owners had waited to see how their pet fared. Unfortunately, she had not done well and had ended up in the hospital on intravenous fluids and intensive care for a few days. With this history, they knew it was imperative to bring the dog to the clinic immediately.

The patient arrived looking very happy and healthy. She had just eaten the chocolate and we were in the ideal time frame for emptying her stomach and avoiding any effects the chocolate might have on her system. I popped an apomorphine tablet inside her lower eyelid and prepared for the anticipated gastric eruption. With a technician holding the patient, I covered the floor with newspapers and we waited.

Within a few minutes, my happy, tail-wagging canine patient began to lap her lips and the expression on her face changed from smiling to apprehensive. Her tail was definitely not wagging now. Predictably, her stomach began to rumble and heave and eventually she brought up a small pile of foamy phlegm that had a distinct chocolate tinge.

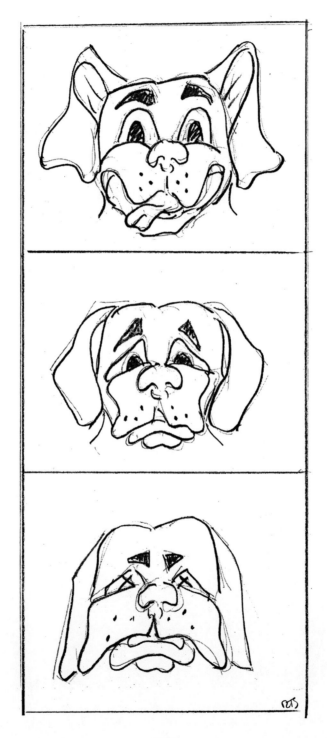

"Great, we're done, let's get out of here," my technician said.

I looked up and realized she had developed a definite green tinge. This was the first time she had seen this scenario acted out and it didn't appear to agree with her. I knew there was more to come, so I quickly excused her and called in our kennel attendant who was a seasoned veteran of such outings.

After a few chuckles at the expense of the neophyte, we spread more clean newspaper and waited. Just when it seemed the apomorphine might have lost its desired effect, the dog stiffened, retched, and emitted a noxious effluvium that featured many brightly colored pieces of silver wrappings. This was more like it! Ready to flush the medication from the dog's eye as soon as it seemed appropriate, I yanked on some plastic gloves and started searching through the mess on the floor. I pulled out wrapper after wrapper. At least the dog had good taste. This wasn't just any chocolate; it was an expensive imported brand. The owner said the dog had eaten almost a full box of bars.

"Three, four, five ... six, seven," I counted as I plucked the virtually intact foil wrappers from the goo. Finally I called out, "Eleven!"

Nothing more was evident and that certainly looked like a boxful of chocolates to me. I felt confident that my patient's stomach was now empty.

"Flush!" I called out.

My helper flushed the dog's eye to remove the medication and within minutes, the dog's face relaxed and her tail started to wag again.

Now there was time to unwind. I looked at my patient's record card. Unbelievably, her previous chocolate encounter had been exactly two years earlier, December 23. I went out to the waiting room to speak with the owners. I advised them that their pet was doing great and would be discharged to their care very shortly.

They were anxious to know if we had gotten all the chocolate out. I assumed my Cheshire cat grin and said, "Ghirardelli dark chocolate?"

They quickly nodded.

"Eleven bars?"

Their eyes widened and they said that would be correct.

"We're done then," I said, "and I have some critical information for you. Every year on December twenty-third, I want you to watch this dog around the clock and lock up any chocolate in the house."

This story is almost too cute and probably not even worth the recounting except for the details. My patient's name was Cocoa. And the breed that would have such a voracious appetite?

That, of course, would be a Labrador Retriever, a chocolate lab, to be exact. You just can't make this stuff up.

CHAPTER 25
A Case of Mistaken Identity

Emergency Vets is, I'm sure, a wonderful and educational television show, but it is not on my list for an evening of entertainment. I hated to disappoint my clients, but after a long day at the clinic, I would not look forward to a busman's holiday of more veterinary clinic angst on the tube. In fact, I watched very little television. Much more interesting to me is the theater. Being in a small town practice was often like having a front row seat at an amateur theater. Every day had new situations and new plots. The cast of characters changed constantly with regional favorites popping up frequently, cameo appearances, and bright new stars appearing every day. Some days were a Shakespearean drama and others were light comedy.

I watched the new client across the examination table as she chattered and cooed over her pet. She was a new player to our stage and a visitor from out of state. She was a huge fan of the Animal Planet channel and seemed to have every episode of their veterinary shows memorized.

My patient was a bright and engaging little poodle. He was just a youngster, not yet a year old. The owners lived in a large metropolitan area, which was evident from their accents. They were outgoing and provided me with all the background information I requested and more. The wife was the conversation leader, and she was obviously the primary bond in the family for the little dog. They were spending some time in our area having a prolonged visit with a family friend. Unfortunately, the friend was allergic to dogs so the husband was staying with the friend while the wife and dog stayed in a local motel. They had been living like this for several weeks and were planning to return home in a few days.

They came to the clinic when they noticed a decrease in the dog's appetite over the span of a few days and repeated vomiting. As I went through my list of questions to gather information, the wife kept jumping ahead, anticipating the next question, or analyzing my reason for posing the question. She was convinced the problem was that the dog had been eating dryer lint. There was a laundry facility at the motel and every time she used it, the dog accompanied her and was obsessed with sucking up the balls of lint that had fallen from the dryer. I decided not to ask why she continued to take the dog with her to the laundry.

Although the intrepid owner felt she clearly had the diagnosis, I continued to plow through my history taking. She fairly bounced from one foot to another and kept proclaiming, "Oooh, I know all about that, I watch the Animal Planet and never miss *Emergency Vets!*"

She quizzed me about my television habits and preferences, hoping that we had seen the same episode. I hated to disappoint her with the truth. I kept this to myself and just told her that I must have missed whichever episode she was discussing. Armed with her media knowledge, she would throw out guesses as to what my diagnosis was going to be or what tests I would call for.

Although this encounter could have been somewhat frustrating, I did not have a full appointment schedule, the dog was a pleasure to work on, and the owners became more entertaining by the moment. They animatedly discussed every small detail of the dog's activities during the last few days and shared their veterinary knowledge acquired during their hours in front of the television screen. I relaxed and decided to let this show unfold. The wife's enthusiasm became contagious, and she went off on several monologues about the trials and tribulations of those amazing "Emergency Vets." I hoped she thought my life was half as exciting or that I was a fraction as capable as those she found so riveting on the television.

I find there are some people who develop like a fine wine and this woman was turning into one of them. What was veterinary practice about if not to learn and grow while serving our patients? Listening to her speech patterns, I was lifted back to my veterinary school days in New York where the majority of my classmates hailed from Long Island. I felt like I had known her for years, although we'd only met that very afternoon. Besides, I had been taken into her circle of TV buddies and she was an ebullient storyteller.

Finally, I realized that my patient was still on the table looking perplexed, and I hadn't even begun to put forth *my* diagnosis. During the physical examination, I had not found anything out of the ordinary. The dog was bright and lively, had no fever, no abdominal pain, or other indication of problems.

I hated to disappoint these charming people. In most cases like this, I would have prescribed some medication to help alleviate the vomiting, suggested a bland diet, and told the owners to come back if the pet did not improve in twenty-four hours. From her chatter, I gathered that this client was expecting a CAT scan, full blood panel, "lytes," bone scans, and more. I decided to compromise. I told her that I had found nothing amiss on physical examination, but thought I should take an X-ray of her pet's abdomen just to be on the safe side. I warned them that dryer lint would not show up on an X-ray but that an obstruction in the gastrointestinal tract often produces abnormal gas patterns and this would be worth pursuing. The wife jumped with excitement and almost clapped her hands with approval. I picked up my patient to move to the radiology room and told the owners I would return with him and the X-ray shortly.

Sometimes we do the right thing for the wrong reasons, and this was certainly one of those times. I had decided to take the X-ray to fulfill the expectations of my client. When the film went up on the view box, I said a little prayer of thanks for being such a grandstander. To my surprise, the poodle had abnormal gas patterns in his bowel. Even worse, there was a fairly large collection of irregular dense material in his colon that looked like dirt. Worst of all, there was a shadow of an obvious foreign body located high up in the intestinal tract. The image showed a darkened, moderately dense oval area attached to a much larger, lighter area shaped like the letter *C*. I could not guess what the dog had eaten, but it definitely looked like something man-made.

I carried the dog back to the room and handed him over to the husband. I had decided to retain some semblance of control in this situation. Since the wife had conducted the bulk of the initial interview, and I realized she had a good sense of humor, I snapped the film up on the view box, stood back, and announced, "You watch *Emergency Vets*. Tell me what you see."

I had fully expected moments of head scratching, a few questions on orientation of organs, or possibly even perplexed silence. She glanced at the film for a few seconds then shouted, "He ate my hearing aid!"

I had to work very hard to keep my mouth from flying open. As soon as she named it, it was clear to me that this probably was what I was seeing. The *C* shaped piece would be the part that coiled back around the ear and the oval was the device itself. I resisted the temptation to put my face next to the dog's belly and ask, "Can you hear me now?"

Hating to be beaten at my own game, I asked what the apparent dirt particles were. Had she seen the dog eating quantities of dirt?

She waved that question aside with her hand and announced, "Oh, that's bathtub caulking. Ever since we moved into the motel room he's been digging at the bathtub and eating the caulking."

That was a good piece of information.

My respect for this woman was growing by leaps and bounds. I may have been studying at the foot of the master. Maybe I should be assigning myself to hours of *Emergency Vets*. It certainly seemed to provide her with an excellent veterinary background.

I explained (probably unnecessarily) that the dog was going to require abdominal exploratory surgery to remove the foreign body. Although most owners receive this kind of news with anxiety and concern, she seemed delighted. She explained that she had been searching high and low for the hearing aid, which was a very expensive model, and she was relieved to know exactly where it was. Fortunately, she had a second appliance and was able to function in the meantime.

She then shook her head and waved a finger at the dog. "And your training has been going so well," she said. "I guess you'll have a vacation for a while until you've recuperated."

I asked what kind of training he was getting, expecting that he was going to obedience school.

"He's being trained as a hearing assistance dog for me," she said.

I took this to be the most extreme case of ensuring job security that I had ever seen.

I admitted my patient, and when the preoperative blood work, intravenous fluid therapy, and sedation were complete, I took him to surgery. There had been some discussion among staff members as to the water resistance of a hearing aid. We were taking bets on the appliance's usefulness after retrieval.

I identified the portion of bowel containing the foreign body and lifted it gently out of the incision. It was difficult to be certain, as I had very little experience with these devices, but the mass seemed too large to be a hearing aid. After packing off the area with sterile gauze, I incised the wall of the bowel over the largest portion of the bulge. To my surprise, out popped the head of a yellow plastic ducky! I manipulated bowel and mass and eventually removed the rest of the yellow plastic duck, which was flat and hollow on one side. It ain't over 'til it's over in our line of investigation.

My patient made a swift and uneventful recovery. By the next morning, he was bouncing in his cage and yelping for breakfast. I was delighted that I could return this cute dog to its owners in such good shape. They would be able to return home on schedule, and I expected the little guy to be back to all his activities in a few weeks. I saved my little twist to the story to surprise the owner when she came to pick up her dog.

When it was time to discharge the poodle, I made sure I was on hand to bid farewell to the garrulous owner. I gave my home care instructions and presented them with the bill for services rendered. I brought out the pup, there were showers of kisses, and hugs, the dog obviously overjoyed to be reunited, and the owners equally delighted to see their healthy pet. I had cleaned up the yellow ducky, and with a dramatic flourish, presented it to the woman for her examination. "And here is what your little culprit actually ate," I announced.

She studied it closely, and then told me it was a decorative trim for the shower curtain rings in the motel bathroom. She guessed that it had fallen while the dog was digging at the tub and he had eaten it.

Suddenly, the mood in the room fell like a cold soufflé. The woman who had not lacked for words just stared at the counter while her husband continued to lavish affection on the poodle. My first thought was that she might be upset with the size of the bill. They were, after all, on vacation and may not have enough funds available on such short notice. I asked her if it was a problem.

"Oh, no, not at all. We have pet health insurance on him and it will cover almost everything," she said.

Still, she was lost in contemplation. I remarked on how well the dog had done and how good his prospects were.

"Yes, I can see he's good as new," she said.

I couldn't stand the tension. I finally asked her what was wrong.

"Well," she said. "Now I have to go back to the darn motel and start looking for my hearing aid again!"

CHAPTER 26
I Knew You Wouldn't Mind

Trying to regain some semblance of poise, I walk toward the waiting room on shaky legs. My breathing is becoming slightly slower and more regular along with my heartbeat. Although my hair appears to have been styled with a Waring blender, I have all ten digits intact. The only blood I have lost is from some long ragged scratches down the inner side of my forearm. It looks like I can count myself as the winner in the last examination room battle. Clutching the precious tube of blood that I have extracted from my unwilling patient, I hear the empty vaccine vials jingling merrily in my pocket. Foolishly, I begin to relax.

Veterinarians are some of the most trusted professionals in the eyes of the American public. I did not make this up. Independent groups have researched and published this fact. Whereas this is very flattering, it can be the bane of our existence. Because we are trusted, clients also perceive us as caring to a fault, and having no other agenda but to serve their pets, regardless of the time that is required or the degree of difficulty. Almost without exception, I have felt compelled to try to fulfill these lofty expectations. Some of my attempts are more successful than others are.

One scenario is universal to all small animal practices. A canine patient is presented that is historically difficult to handle. The task requires the patient be muzzled. I know this, the owner knows this, and unfortunately, the patient knows this. Any dog that requires a muzzle quickly learns the drill, and it is a rare dog that sits quietly as the muzzle is applied. There is no discomfort involved, but the dog knows well that it is losing its power the minute the device is in place. Dogs definitely ascribe to the old saw, "Fool me once, shame on you; fool me twice, shame on me."

Regardless of the size or breed, German Shepherd or Chihuahua, they know what's coming and they do their best to avoid the inevitable. It is an intricate ballet between the doctor and patient, during which the doctor strives to deftly maneuver the muzzle into place and quickly secure it while maintaining some appearance of self-confidence. Meanwhile, the patient bobs and weaves and feints while snapping at the hated appendages. The quicker this process is completed, the better the outcome is for all concerned.

Once the muzzle is in place, we try to accomplish our assigned tasks as smoothly and efficiently as possible—physical examination, vaccination, blood draw, whatever is called for during that particular visit. I have learned to ask the owner if anything further requires my attention. If the answer is no, I quickly slip off the muzzle and surreptitiously take a quick step away from the dog, for I have met just a few who do hold a grudge.

The next step is the one all veterinarians dread. Just as we exit the exam room and approach the reception area, the owner will suddenly stop, turn around, and say, "Oh, Doctor, I forgot. I know you won't mind, but could you please cut his nails?"

That this always occurs in front of an expectant crowd of well-wishers in the waiting room makes it all the more difficult to decline.

The assembled multitude smile benignly, gently nod their heads, secure in the knowledge that the wish will be granted. Certainly, their trusted veterinarian wouldn't want this 110-pound snarling Rottweiler to suffer one more minute with toenails that are at least one-quarter of an inch too long, would she? Resistance is pointless. I slowly turn and retrace my recent escape path back into the examination room, grateful that none of my clients can read minds.

Act Two of this play is always much more dramatic than Act One, and involves lots of choreography. Now wary of the muzzle, the dog will not allow it anywhere near his head. There is a great deal of jousting back and forth for position in the room, narrow escapes, and in the case of the smaller breeds, often evacuation of bodily substances on the floor, table, and doctor. Newly trimmed nails, now rapier sharp around the edges, flail with all four paws wind milling in the air. Any human flesh that comes in the way is quickly shredded.

Would I mind? Of course not!

***

Full of enthusiasm, I enter the large equine boarding stable on my first call of the morning. Scanning my list of requests at this facility, my jolly mood quickly dampened. One of my patients needs his sheath cleaned. He's a sweet old gelding and a delight to work on. But it's Saturday morning. This promises to be very, very bad.

A visit by the large animal veterinarian is always a popular event and draws in young horse owners who might be visiting their beloved animals at the time. They all share the image of every practitioner of veterinary medicine being as saintly as James Herriot was. Would that we were!

One of the most heinous tasks in equine work, at least by my standards, is cleaning out geldings' sheaths. The horse owning public does not commonly acknowledge this requirement of equine hygiene. Geldings accumulate various amounts of thick, greasy, malodorous discharge high in the folds of their prepuce. Some horses have no problem with this, but others develop a "bean" or concretion that impedes the flow of urine. Regardless, the proper maintenance of a gelding, especially as he ages, dictates that the structure be manually cleansed on a regular basis. This involves reaching in with a long sleeved plastic obstetrical glove, using a disinfecting scrub, and gently scraping and loosening all the nasty accumulation. Inevitably, the glove tears, making it worthless as a shield, but veterinarians go through the motions of putting one on, sporting a positive attitude and high expectations.

It is amazing how far up this cavity extends, often encasing half the forearm. Some horses stand docilely for this procedure while others need sedation. The combination of being a disgusting job made dangerous by flying hind feet always lends drama to the moment. Finally, no amount of hand washing eradicates the lingering odor for the rest of the day. The veterinarian is left with olfactory memories of a job well done. The spouse need not ask what you did that day; they know.

When some intrepid soul requested having his or her steed's sheath cleaned, I always shuddered with dread. I had no problem caring for the one horse, but if housed with others, a crowd would often gather, and I could see the lights going on over various owners' heads as I hoed out matter from my patient's inner regions. I would silently pray that most of them owned mares.

But of course, that was never the case and soon someone would say, "Gee, Doc, when you're through, I know you wouldn't mind doing my horse. He's never had this done, and I'm sure he really needs it."

Heads would start nodding all around and before I could open my mouth, it was like Sunday morning at the deli with patrons lined up waving their numbers at the counter. I would be in for a long morning introducing all my new charges to the joys of a clean sheath and my previous schedule of calls would be history.

***

Slowly I turned my head, unable to comprehend the request that had just been made of me. I wouldn't mind *what*?

The horse owner stared at me phlegmatically. Realizing that I was doing James Herriot a grave disservice, and that this client would be the one to skew the polls about trusting their veterinarians over all other health professionals, I refused.

The man in question had made an emergency call during the night for his mare that had foaled and had not been able to pass her placenta. This is a serious condition in horses and requires immediate attention. I did not have much experience with the situation, and I was filled with trepidation. The mare was anxious with her newborn, uncomfortable and distressed. I was reluctant to sedate her for fear of interfering with her bonding with her foal. The procedure is to extricate manually the placenta from the patient's uterus. An internal obstetrical examination requires the veterinarian be in prime striking range of the hindquarters, and the mare can hardly be blamed for objecting strenuously to the ministration.

I had no previous experience with this mare, and I certainly was not meeting her under ideal circumstances. She was not at her best. We arranged a setup where she was blocked on both sides from swinging around, and we placed a row of hay bales behind her so that if she did kick, the bales would be between her hooves and me. This worked fairly well. That is to say, I survived the event with no odd horseshoe shaped indentations on my body. My heart was pounding from exertion and adrenaline as I meticulously lifted the placenta from its attachments and slowly removed it. It was crucial not to tear the delicate structure, so that a portion is left behind. This can have catastrophic repercussions for the mother. Toxic infection and founder of the mare's hooves can result.

Sighing with relief, I had begun to lay out the placenta on the barn floor to check its integrity and confirm that I had removed all of it. It was 4:00 AM. I was filthy and tired in a wired-up way that veterinarians are in these situations. We are sleep deprived, maybe overly caffeinated, certainly maxed out on adrenalin, and just about ready to hit the big downslide of the fatigue roller coaster. At this moment, the stable owner announced, "Well, Doc, I was going to call you for an appointment soon, but since you're already here, and I won't have to pay another call charge, I know you won't mind cleaning the sheaths of a few geldings I have right now?"

I had foolishly thought he would appreciate the fact that I had dragged myself out of bed to come to his mare's aid and was able to treat her successfully. If it was going to be all about the money anyway, I decided to stand my ground. I politely declined and suggested that he schedule that for another day. He looked disgruntled but accepted my decision. And my clear memory of this incident sticks with me most because I still feel a little guilty about it.

***

Why had I answered the telephone? I was not on call and so was not responsible for emergencies at the clinic. Before I could explore that line of thinking any longer, a major contraction grabbed my attention, and I valiantly cast about for whatever object that I had chosen for my focal point in my Lamaze class. Too late to catch the wave, I began to huff and pant like a spent racehorse.

I was in labor with our first child. I live in a small town and my presence here is no secret to the residents. Although my home phone number is unlisted, it still manages to circulate through some devious underground network. I can run, but I cannot hide.

My pregnancy had been delightfully uneventful. When I reached the time of delivery, I learned the true meaning of labor. When I finally went into serious contractions, it was a Saturday afternoon and I was riding out the siege at home with my husband. I had started doing my childbirth breathing exercises and speculating how much longer we should wait before heading to the hospital when the phone rang. Foolishly, I had answered it.

On the line was a local fellow, Keith, whose dog I had seen a few times at the clinic. The man was quite distressed and hard to understand, but I appreciated his anxiety when it became clear that his dog was having multiple seizures. This is a difficult situation and always bound to upset even the staunchest individual. I was unable to break into his description of what he was witnessing, but finally he had to pause for breath. I quickly explained that seizures that come in series are dangerous and that he needed to call our clinic to alert the doctor on duty and get the pet into the clinic immediately.

Without further thought, he again launched into his emotional description of the dog's activities and what he suspected was causing them. Again I waited for him to draw a breath (meanwhile wondering if I needed to be doing a focused breath as I felt a contraction coming), and I reiterated that he needed to hang up now, call the emergency number, and the doctor on call would see him immediately.

Undeterred and clearly confused, he informed me that I should remember having seen the dog in the past. I told him I certainly did remember his dog, but that I was having a baby now and would be unable to do any veterinary work for a while. He said he knew I was going to have a baby and extended his congratulations, but then he assured me that he didn't think it would take me very long to treat his dog and that he would be glad to help.

"Keith, I am having a baby. I am having this baby *now*! I am having contractions right now while I'm talking to you. I can't possibly leave the house," I firmly informed him through clenched teeth as I let a contraction get ahead of me.

Poor oblivious Keith responded, "Then I know you wouldn't mind if I just brought the dog over to your house for you to have a quick look, would you?"

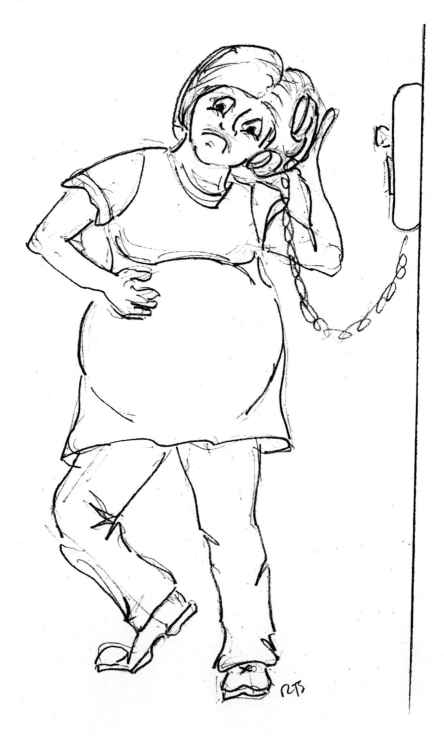

CHAPTER 27
Living with Wildlife

"Real doctors treat more than one species," so states my favorite T-shirt.

Embracing this concept, I was always happy to minister to any needy animal to the best of my ability. The challenge of dealing with the unknown, the unmanageable, and often the unappreciative was very attractive to me. When presented with injured wildlife, I would do my best to return them to health, although they never thought to call ahead for appointments and generally showed up at the most inopportune times. They are as close as I would ever come to my initial dream of treating patients that present themselves at the clinic door with no complicating human owners. Of course, like unwanted houseguests, they also arrive penniless and demanding.

***

"Just give me a minute to finish this X-ray and then I'll have a look at it," I said. Hurrying through a busy morning of appointments one day, I had decided to sneak in a quick radiograph on one of my patients when my husband poked his head around the door of the X-ray room. The local game warden was in the waiting room. A motorist had reported an injured Great Blue Heron next to the road. The warden had gathered up the bird and although he thought it was probably beyond help, had brought it in for my evaluation.

Sweating under the weight of the cumbersome lead apron we are required to wear while taking films, I wondered if I would ever find a moment to myself on this crazy morning. John reappeared at the door cradling a large, limp mass of shiny feathers in his arms.

"I think it's too late, anyway," he said as he regretfully looked down at his burden.

The bird's neck and head dangled limply, looking like some exotic snake. The heron has a body the size of a small turkey and the rest of it is somewhat reminiscent of scaffolding erected in haste and never fully fleshed out. It was the first time I had seen one so close, and certainly the first time I had ever seen one other than flying like a pterodactyl or precariously balancing on a stilt-like leg. But there was no time to waste in idle inspection of this wonder of nature. I had to finish my first task before quickly moving on to a thorough examination of the bird.

Holding up a finger, I said, "Just give me one second, I'll be right there," and swept by John and the bird, anxious to move my current patient off the X-ray table.

Suddenly, I felt a stab in my arm. I grabbed my arm and screamed, bringing all sound and motion in the room to a halt. There were four people in the room and every single one of us was standing with our mouths open in a huge *O* and our eyes popping. A small stream of blood was trickling from my upper arm, but nobody had seen the cause.

Then John burst out laughing. For reasons I don't understand, he often finds my minor incidences of bodily harm amusing. He proceeded to explain what happened.

As I rushed past the heron, purportedly at death's door, the bird had suddenly sprung to life, whipped out its previously limp neck, speared me with its beak, and then resumed its death trance so quickly that nobody had seen it and John had no chance to react. At least it was clear that it was too early to call the coroner for this patient.

We later determined the heron had suffered a concussion, presumably from being struck by a vehicle. I entertained myself with figuring out scaled-down doses of medications I would administer to one of my domestic patients in such a situation and administered them. The bird made a good recovery in just a few days. During this time, we kept him in a large kennel in the treatment area. We kept busy with trips to the local pet store to buy goldfish and guppies sacrificed in the name of Caduceus in a large water-filled dog dish in the heron's kennel.

The heron felt well enough to slurp down this buffet.

Soon we were faced with the dilemma of releasing the bird. After an injury, there is no guarantee that a bird can immediately fend for itself in the wild. It is best to put the bird in rehabilitation for a period of time, a wildlife halfway house, so to speak. I called the Vermont Institute of Natural Science to arrange for them to take the heron for his rehabilitation. The phone call confirmed that I was born more than a little lucky.

When I told the rehabilitator that we had a Great Blue Heron that I had been treating, she quickly broke into the conversation. "You be careful with that bird! A Golden Eagle can maim you, but a Great Blue Heron can kill you. They catch fish by spearing them with the point of their beak. They are extremely fast and coordinated. They usually aim at eyes, and there have been incidences of people killed immediately by a heron spearing them in the eye and penetrating their brain. Anytime you handle the bird, make sure one person is responsible for the bird's head and another handles the body. Make sure you trust the person on the head and that no matter what, they won't let go of it."

After returning my dropped jaw to a more normal position, I

opted to omit the part of the story about the heron's admission to the hospital. I have had many reluctant patients, but very few who fired the first salvo like this one did.

***

"So what should we call him?" I asked when I realized the crow I was examining would be coming home with us. Without missing a beat, John said, "Edgar Allen Crow!" And so Edgar, that had apparently fledged too early, became our houseguest that eventually overstayed his welcome.

Although he was a fairly large bird, Edgar was still unable to fly. Very vulnerable, he needed a safe haven to live until he could navigate the air. We have a flight pen at our house that was appropriate for him. Edgar was charming, but we did our best to keep contact to twice-daily checks on him and feeding him to avoid having him imprint on us. He adored cat food, which was readily available and easy to dole out. It was nutritionally balanced for this category of bird, so he was low maintenance.

We would watch Edgar from the house and monitor his progress learning to navigate as his flight feathers grew in. Hopping followed experimental wing flapping, and then he'd be off the ground for a few seconds. Eventually, he could fly up into a small pine tree in the flight pen and perch reliably. During this entire period, we did not interact with him or spend time in or around the pen. We were his meal ticket and nothing more.

Finally it was clear that Edgar was ready for the big world. Feeling like an overly protective mother, I reluctantly opened the door and we herded Edgar out of the pen. We did this just before his usual mealtime. In case he ran into trouble, we thought we could probably entice him back into the cage with food. Our worries were unwarranted, and he flew from the lower branches of one tree to the next, obviously enjoying his new freedom. As dusk approached, I worried that he didn't know enough about predators to spend the night outside, so we easily lured him back in with his favorite cat kibble. With him safe in the sanctuary, I slept well.

We began a regular routine of letting Edgar out in the morning and allowing him back in the flight pen in the evening. It soon became clear that he was a big boy and needed to stay outside and find his own way. John and I made a pact: our boy was ready to go to college and we were not going to let him back in, no matter what. Unfortunately, Edgar had become part of the Boomerang Generation and didn't care for our plans.

Late one afternoon I was riding my horse in the riding ring. Shortly after starting my ride, Edgar joined us. He flew from post to post, crying and complaining piteously. Whining toddlers could learn from the exhibit Edgar put on. He was not to be ignored. Not able to concentrate, and my poor horse completely shaken by this cheeky bird, I decided a little trail ride was in order. As I had hoped, Edgar followed, but to my dismay, he followed all the way back to the house, too, and greeted me from a position high on top of the netting of the flight cage.

This pattern continued for days. Our lives were plagued with this complaining, intrusive ex-houseguest, demanding food and lodging. Flapping around us, regardless of our activities, cawing and begging for kitty treats, he was always present. In my mind's eye, he was the avian version of the lanky teenager hanging over the refrigerator with the door open, decrying that "There's nothing to eat in this house. I'm *starving.*" I can only speak for myself, but there were a few times when I folded and snuck a little cat food out to him, though I made certain nobody saw me. If he was a smart as I think he was, he probably was working the crowd sequentially and doing quite well for himself.

One day, I realized there were several crows near our house, and it was impossible to pick out Edgar. I'll never be sure, but I hope that he found a nice gang to hang out with and he had a good life. A group of three crows often visits us in the spring and I have dubbed them The Three Amigos. Maybe Edgar is one of them.

***

Although wildlife houseguests can be rude for not leaving, others have been rude for their manner of leaving. A beaver brought into our clinic one winter was extremely thin and poor. It had been found on a major road, apparently frozen out of his lodge. We decided to do what we could to fortify him, and if he recovered, to harbor him until spring.

The beaver was full of parasites, but he responded well to worm treatment and began to improve. We named him Cleaver the Beaver and took him home to spend the winter in our barn. There he had a large horse stall to himself. We kept water available for drinking and would regularly bring him a big pile of sticks. I always felt mean as I passed out appetizing food to dogs, cats, and horses and then dumped a pile of sticks in Cleaver's stall, but beavers have a diet that consists of the soft layer under the bark on trees.

Winter passed and Cleaver seemed to be doing well. His only interaction was an occasional hiss before he retreated to a corner when we delivered food to him. Sticks and twigs presented one day would be retrieved a day or two later with the bark neatly stripped off. This was an unusual boarder.

Finally, the weather began to warm slightly and water in the local stream began to gurgle with life. Before we even thought about plans for Cleaver's release, he took matters into his own hands, or rather, his own teeth. Walking into the barn, I was shocked to see a big semicircle carved out of Cleaver's sliding stall door. Indeed, he had been a busy little beaver. The window in the stall was too high for him to look out, the stream was too far away to hear, and the weather was only slightly warmer than it had been, yet he knew his time had come.

We herded Cleaver into a pet carrier and headed for the local stream, a perfect beaver habitat. We were quite excited and pleased that our attempt to rescue the huge rodent was looking to be a success. Certainly, Cleaver must be excited as well, or so we thought.

When we had carried the cage down to the stream and opened the door, Cleaver quickly exited. No long last meaningful look from his beady little eyes, not even a token hostess gift offered. He hissed in his ominous way once, did not look back, and slipped into the water. We never saw him again. In my opinion, his mother had not done a very good job raising that young man. I scratched him off my future guest list and regretted not having required a security deposit.

CHAPTER 28
The Other End of the Leash

"It's a *job*?" It was inconceivable to me at the time that anyone would actually be paid to perform such wonderful tasks.

The trip to the "animal doctor" with my parents had shaken my world. I was fascinated beyond anything my limited vocabulary could convey. Certainly, the man in the short white jacket must be having the best time anyone could imagine. Handling animals of all sorts every day and being called upon to help them in their times of need seemed to me a mystical, special honor that must be bestowed upon only a few worthy individuals. I had found my superhero. Then my parents told me that it was a job. After mulling this over for quite awhile, I asked if people were *paid* to perform these wonderful tasks. When they answered in the affirmative, it was probably the most exciting news of my young life. Being paid to play every day? That's when I decided that veterinary medicine would be my life's work. The details of how one managed to qualify for the white coat would come later.

The fact that very few women were in the field at the time did nothing to swerve me in my determined pursuit of the prize. This may seem as dedicated feminism or even activism, but in truth, I was merely stubborn. When I fix on a goal, I develop what borders on tunnel vision. Unless I am smote directly on the head with harsh details of reality, I will persistently, sometimes annoyingly, continue on my predestined path. My parents never pushed nor did they discourage my ambitions. They probably felt it would run its course and let fate play out. With hindsight, I applaud their decision to humor me.

School went very well for me, and I was comfortable in the courses that might bring me closer to my destiny. It was not a dream, because I was so certain of its realization; it was just a matter of time. As I progressed, I was often asked what I wanted to do in life. When I related my plans, people treated me with patience, but nobody ever gave me the impression that they thought it was possible. Friends often counseled that I should consider being a human physician, a more realistic goal since my grades were so good. My ironically naive comment at the time was, "I don't even like people, why would I want to be a human doctor?" Obviously, this was an exaggeration full of teenage swagger and meant to shock, but little did I know how important this would be later in my career.

The truth is, after more than thirty years as a veterinarian, I now realize that a large part of my profession involves the care and maintenance of the Homo sapiens responsible for my patients. All the skills and knowledge I obtained at school targeted the animal population. There was no preparation for the people in the animals' lives. This I learned in the field and it has provided me with wonderful experiences, priceless memories, deep frustration, and many laughs. After all these years, I am realizing that the human animal may be the most interesting of all. How amazing it is for me to think that I have been studying and practicing for all this time and been oblivious to the course title.

People have been kind beyond measure, awesomely dedicated, and splendidly appreciative over the years. They have also been quirky, infuriating, and sometimes behave in inexplicable fashion. There is no model of an ideal client. This keeps practice a true art and makes every day a challenge. I have had the opportunity to bond with people for many years, see them form families, raise them, and sometimes even watch the families disintegrate or move away. I share their bereavement over the loss of their pets as well as their partners and family. We have laughed together, cried together, and occasionally glared over an examination table or stall door in total mutual exasperation. Sometimes I feel as though I am speaking a foreign language to them and other times I have the eerie feeling that the owner is capable of reading my mind. I look back with pride that I have never experienced a typical day.

My love for animals is lifelong and deep-seated, but without a genuine affection and appreciation for the vast array of humanity, I would never have been able to enjoy my chosen career. The gods must certainly be having a hearty laugh on my account.